A. Satinwood secretary bookcase, with inlaid and painted decoration; c. 1790.
Victoria and Albert Museum.

SHERATON FURNITURE

by

RALPH FASTNEDGE

ANTIQUE COLLECTORS' CLUB

ISBN 0 907462 47 2

First published in 1962
by Faber and Faber Limited
and reprinted in 1983 for the
Antique Collectors' Club
by the Antique Collectors' Club Ltd.

British Library CIP Data

Fastnedge, Ralph
  Sheraton furniture
  1. Furniture — England — History
  I. Title
  749.22   NK2529

Printed in England by
Baron Publishing, Church Street, Woodbridge, Suffolk

ACKNOWLEDGEMENTS

The illustrations of furniture from the Royal Collections are reproduced by gracious permission of H.M. the Queen (Plates 31, 35, 47).

Grateful acknowledgement is made to the owners of pieces illustrated, and for the use of photographs, as follows: Director and Secretary, Victoria and Albert Museum (Colour Plates A–D, Plates 2–3, 6–7, 9–12, 15, 20, 24–27, 36A and B, 38–39, 40B, 41, 43–45, 48–50, 53, 56, 57A and B, 66–67, 70–71, 88, 90A and B, 91, 95, 96A); Trustees of the Lady Lever Art Gallery (Plates 22–23, 28A and B, 30, 32A and B, 33A, 40A, 52, 62, 73, 94A and B); Messrs. Waring & Gillow, Ltd., Lancaster (Plates 18A and B, 19A and B, 58–59, 78–79, 80A and B, 81A and B, 92A and B, 93A and B); City Museum and Art Gallery, Birmingham (Plate 75); Royal Pavilion Committee, Brighton Corporation (Plates 17, 34, 55, 77); Trustees of the British Museum (Plate 96B); Metropolitan Museum of Art, New York (Plates 8, 29A and B); Sir John Soane's Museum (Plates 5, 13, 16); Public Libraries, Museum and Art Gallery, Stockton-on-Tees and Tees Conservancy Commission, Middlesbrough (Plate 4); Trustees of the Wallace Collection (Plate 21); Messrs. Norman Adams, Ltd., London, S.W.3 (Plates 60–61); *Apollo*, London, W.1. (Plate 76); Messrs. Ayer & Co. Ltd., Bath (Plates 14, 33B, 51, 65, 68, 83); Messrs. H. C. Baxter & Sons, London, S.W.5 (Plate 87); *The Connoisseur*, London, W.1. (Plates 54, 63, 86); Messrs. M. Harris & Sons, London, W.C.1. (Plates 37A, B, C and D, 64); Messrs. Jeremy, Ltd., London, S.W.3 (Plates 33C, 69, 82); Messrs. Phillips of Hitchin, Ltd. (Plates 46, 72, 74, 84–85).

It is regretted that it has not been possible in all cases to verify the present ownership of pieces.

Acknowledgement is due to Messrs. Jonathan Cape, Ltd., for permission to quote extracts from *Sophie in London, 1786*, translated from the German by Clare Williams, 1933, and to the Cambridge University Press for material from *A Frenchman in England, 1784*, translated by S. C. Roberts, 1933.

The author is grateful for assistance of various kinds considerately given by Dr. G. Chandler, City Librarian, Liverpool; Mr. R. Jackson, Director, Messrs.

ACKNOWLEDGEMENTS

Waring & Gillow, Ltd., Lancaster, and Mr. H. Palliser; Mr. W. R. Jeudwine; Mr. H. Jones and Mr. G. R. Griffiths, of Photographic Research, Unilever, Ltd., Port Sunlight; Mr. Clifford Musgrave, Director of the Brighton Public Libraries, Museums, and the Royal Pavilion; the Rev. Dr. E. A. Payne, General Secretary of the Baptist Union of Great Britain and Ireland; Mr. L. G. G. Ramsey, Editor of *The Connoisseur*; Mr. A. J. Raper, Church Secretary, Church Hill Baptist Chapel, Walthamstow; the late Lord Strathcona and Mount Royal; Sir John Summerson, Curator of Sir John Soane's Museum; Mr. T. B. Watkin, of Messrs. John Broadwood & Sons, Ltd.; and Messrs. Browns of Liverpool, Photographers. He is specially indebted to Mr. Keith Andrews and Miss Mary Bennett; Miss Joan Newton; Mr. John Lowe, Editor of this series; and, finally, to his wife, for her work of collaboration.

CONTENTS

9

ILLUSTRATIONS

COLOUR PLATES

MONOCHROME PLATES
at the end of the book

ILLUSTRATIONS

INTRODUCTION

'The upholder', according to the author of *The London Tradesman* (1747), 'was originally a species of Taylor, but by degrees has crept over his Head, and set up as a connoisseur in every article that belongs to a House. He employs journeymen in his own proper calling, cabinet-makers, glass grinders, looking-glass framers, carvers for chairs, Testers and Posts for Beds, the Woollen Draper, the mercer, the Linen Draper and several species of smiths and a vast army of tradesmen of the other mechanic branches.'

By the turn of the century, it may be estimated that some two or three hundred makers of furniture had workshops in London. The majority, probably, were of some standing and were able to supply to order goods of graded qualities at widely differing prices, though their shops varied greatly in character and size. Many large firms, combining the several trades of cabinet-maker, upholder (upholsterer), gilder, etc., were in a position to supply from stock almost any article of household furniture — and to undertake interior decoration. Some adopted the designation 'cabinet-makers and upholders'; others that of 'cabinet-makers' or 'upholders'. Seddon's, of Aldersgate Street, to name one outstanding firm, employed about four hundred specialist workmen and carried an enormous stock (see pages 33–34).

The majority of cabinet-makers had showrooms attached to their workshops, where they displayed and sold their own furniture. But there were in existence a not inconsiderable number of retail shops, or 'Cabinet Warehouses', and these, to borrow a phrase used in Mortimer's *Universal Director* of 1763, sold 'ready-made Furniture bought of the real artist'. Their proprietors did not execute work themselves, 'or employ workmen under their direction'. They bought, perhaps, from self-employed journeymen, working in their own homes, or from smaller workshops having little or no trade with the general public.

Soon after 1800 the journeyman cabinet-maker was receiving about four or five shillings a day. There had been a very considerable rise in wages during the last decade of the eighteenth century, due to changed economic conditions brought about by the French war. Journeymen were paid either a daily wage or 'by the piece'. The latter practice was quite common — hence the need for and popularity of *The Cabinet-Makers' London Book of Prices*, a trade manual, first published in 1788 (see pages 16–18).

The best London-made furniture, dating from the closing decades of the eighteenth century, has great technical accomplishment and the quality of workmanship apparent in innumerable surviving pieces is very high. Such furniture was in general unsurpassed elsewhere, or at other periods. Furniture was then being made in greater variety and quantity to satisfy a wider public eager to acquire for their houses pieces in the newest style. Many more people required fashionable, good furniture, and the prices demanded by craftsmen for their products were low, at least up to the times succeeding the French war, which had 'doubled the cost and trebled the difficulty of genteel living'. The distinction that formerly had existed between furniture made for the great houses and that made for the well-to-do was diminishing. New tools[1] were favoured, with ways of working that were less laborious and cheaper, but cabinet-makers had not yet adopted woodworking machinery, nor was mass production in being.

The London shops were centred to some extent in small, well-defined areas or certain streets. Cabinet-makers worked in close and convenient proximity to one another — in Soho, for example, particularly in Wardour Street, or at addresses in St. Martin's Lane and the 'Oxford Road'. There was, understandably, a tendency for the trade to move westwards from the City to the more fashionable side of the town. Gillow's of Lancaster, when taking premises in London, chose a site at '176 Oxford Road', which was then at the north-western fringe of development. The new thoroughfare of Piccadilly contained several shops of note. St. Paul's Churchyard, however, remained an active quarter.

English furniture is largely anonymous: a very small proportion of the quantity of furniture surviving can be identified as being the work of an individual maker or as having originated from a particular workshop. Stamped or marked pieces, bearing a maker's name, are rare. English cabinet-makers, unlike the French *maîtres ébénistes* of the eighteenth century who formed a closed fraternity and who were required by law (after 1741) to use a stamp, did not sign their work. Gillow's of Lancaster provides a notable exception; the name of this firm is often to be found on case furniture dating from the 1790's onwards (Plate 61). Although,

---

[1] A contemporary observer, Sophie von la Roche (see p. 33), refers to new tools, 'manufactured in Birmingham . . . as most valuable and beneficent inventions'.

throughout the century, some makers (particularly those in or near St. Paul's Churchyard) were in the habit of advertising their businesses by pasting printed labels on furniture, usually on the insides of drawers, the practice was never general and fell gradually into disuse; and it is significant that labels bearing the names of such prominent makers as Chippendale, and Vile and Cobb have not come to light. Satisfactory attributions can occasionally be made on the evidence of original bills or receipts which have been kept together with the furniture to which they relate. Attempts to assign furniture to makers on stylistic grounds have had some degree of success, but the procedure is difficult and findings are uncertain unless borne out by documentary or other evidence.

The position is obscured rather than clarified by the existence of the pattern books, despite their value — especially for furniture made in the last quarter of the century. Much of our information on the period is drawn from two famous books of designs: *The Cabinet-Maker and Upholsterer's Guide*, by George Hepplewhite, which was published posthumously in 1788 and contains 'nearly three hundred different patterns for furniture', and *The Cabinet-Maker and Upholsterer's Drawing-Book*, by Thomas Sheraton, which succeeded it. Both are comprehensive and extremely useful works, and facsimile reprints of the third editions were issued in the late 1890's. The designs were then and afterwards studied by collectors and others interested in the subject, but their approach was credulous and the conclusions reached were wholly mistaken: Hepplewhite and Sheraton were advanced as major figures, dominating the design of furniture at this time, and were credited with the actual manufacture of a high proportion of surviving pieces. Fine furniture, if approximately of the right date, was attributed indiscriminately to them. Such furniture did not necessarily bear any correspondence with their designs. No count was taken of the fact that pattern books were issued largely for the benefit of workmen, that they were trade catalogues, intended to be of service to 'Countrymen and Artisans, whose distance from the metropolis makes even an imperfect knowledge of its improvements acquired with much trouble and expence', and to lesser London makers who did not employ a designer but were content to follow others' lead: nor was it considered relevant that scores of master craftsmen, working contemporaneously in London, were producing furniture on very similar lines.

No single piece of furniture has in fact yet been identified as having been made by either Hepplewhite or Sheraton, and curiously few extant pieces are directly and closely related to their book models. 'Book pieces', as they are called, are rare, and most are of a simplified or modified character (Plates 8, 10, 40A, 46, 54, 64, 76, 83, 87). The leading makers (and it is their work that usually is documented, and hence is to be identified) would have been unwilling to reproduce published designs unless to special order.

Hepplewhite was a lesser, even insignificant, member of the trade, working in a not very fashionable quarter of the town (his business was at Redcross Street, St. Giles's, Cripplegate, and was carried on after his death by his widow, trading as A. Hepplewhite & Co.); and Sheraton, in the eyes of those of his fellows who knew of him, was a poverty-stricken drawing master and designer, who eked out a living by 'his exertions as an author' and who did not even possess a workshop of his own.

'Hepplewhite' and 'Sheraton' remain, however, terms generally used to describe furniture in the neo-classic style of the 1780's and 1790's, and these labels are to some extent interchangeable, for the two men shared common ground, although Hepplewhite had died in 1786, when Sheraton was in his middle thirties. The *Guide*, however, was sufficiently popular and useful to run into a third, revised edition in 1794 and inevitably faced comparison with the newly completed *Drawing Book*. That Sheraton was not unmindful of the competition is evidenced by his ungenerous references, which scarcely can have been disinterested, to Hepplewhite and to the obsolete character of some of the designs. He ignored Hepplewhite's having laid no claim to originality, his having omitted 'articles, whose recommendation was mere novelty'. The *Guide* provides in fact an admirable summary of fashions prevailing in the 1780's; and it is of some interest that, at a time of rapid change, it should have merited reprinting. The reason may well lie in the reluctance of the majority of cabinet-makers to abandon established, proven forms. The popularity of another work, *The Cabinet-Makers' London Book of Prices*, which first appeared in 1788, and was reissued in 1793, 1803 and at various other dates in the nineteenth century, would seem to confirm that this was indeed the case with one section of the trade (Plate 2).

This latter publication, sponsored by the London Society of Cabinet-Makers, differs in some essentials from the *Guide* and the *Drawing Book*: it is primarily a manual prepared for the guidance of workmen, and the costs in labour and material of articles of cabinet furniture then in general production are set out in exact detail. The directions for costing are comprehensive and of a technical nature and are by no means confined to those pieces of furniture for which designs are given in the plates. The introduction to the second edition (1793) carries an interesting statement to the effect that these directions, as given

B. Painted satinwood armchair, probably by Seddon's; *c.* 1790.
Victoria and Albert Museum.

formerly, were not 'clear enough to prevent different constructions being put on them both by journeymen and their employers, as their different interests might suggest', that disputes had been frequent and 'in some cases, almost ir-reconcileable'. Both parties are thereupon requested to be 'particular in making themselves acquainted' with a new 'General Explanation' of the rules for costing. Secondly, the *Book of Prices* deals only with cabinet work: it is addressed to the cabinet-maker, and not to the upholder or chair-maker; its range is limited by the exclusion of such articles as beds, chairs and settees, stuffed and plain.

Sheraton praises the work, to which he refers in his preface to the *Drawing Book* as 'a quarto book of different pieces of furniture, with the Cabinet-maker's London Book of Prices'; 'considering that it did not make its appearance under the title of a Book of Designs, but only to illustrate the prices', he states, 'it certainly lays claim to merit, and does honour to the publishers.'

The leading spirit in the undertaking had been Thomas Shearer, and the majority of the plates bear his name. His designs are sound and workman-like, competently drawn and never ostentatious. 'Whether', comments Sheraton, at the expense of the *Guide*, 'they [the designers] had the advantage of seeing Heppelwhite's book before theirs was published I know not; but it may be observed, with justice, that their designs are more fashionable and useful than his, in proportion to their number. . . . I doubt not but they were capable of doing more than Heppelwhite has done, without the advantage of seeing his book: and it may be, for any thing I know, that the advantage was given on their side.'

Sheraton's commendation of Shearer may be taken at face value. He admired the designs and would seem to have put them to good use when preparing material for the *Drawing Book*.

The second edition of the *Book of Prices*, with 29 plates, of which 17 at least must be given to Shearer, contains also 6 by 'Hepplewhite' and 3 by Casement;[1] there are, in all, 49 designs for furniture, with plans and various small details such as patterns for glazing bars or profiles of mouldings. Some designs, as is customarily to be found in the pattern books, are presented with variations — alternative forms for the pediment of a bookcase or the disposition of drawers in a writing table are embodied in the one drawing. Shearer's designs, without exception, are dated 1788 and are therefore reprints; they include library and bureaux bookcases (Plate 66), writing and dressing tables, harlequin tables, side-

---

[1] Casement figures as a subscriber to the first edition of the *Drawing Book*, wherein he is recorded as a cabinet-maker of London; nothing otherwise is known of his life or work.

boards (Plate 41), dressing and basin stands and other articles of bedroom furniture (Plates 67, 90B). Those bearing the name 'Hepplewhite' or 'Heppelwhite' (presumably supplied by the firm A. Hepplewhite & Co.) are new, and dated 1792 or 1793. The draughtsman, whoever he may have been, would seem to have sought novel forms, for among the articles included are a Carlton House table, a gentleman's social table (Plate 45) — a wine table of horseshoe shape, of which a simpler version had been given by Shearer — and a kidney-shaped knee-hole writing table (Plate 45); but the last plate, with forty-five details — 'profiles' of 'claws', 'top mouldings for claws', 'terms for claws' and standards for tripods, etc. — is particularly informative (Plate 49). Of Casement's plates, also new, two are devoted to patterns for glazing bars and the third to 'profiles' of legs — adaptable for cellarets, for card, Pembroke, chamber or work tables, for dining and pier tables and sideboards (Plate 48).

The neo-classic style of the last quarter of the eighteenth century, inaugurated by Adam and other architects, had its roots in the revived interest in the antique which had in part been inspired by excavations of classical remains made at Herculaneum and Pompeii earlier in the century. The neo-classic style was in distinct contrast with that of the preceding period: as Adam remarks in the *Works in Architecture*, in 1778, 'we have not only met with the approbation of our employers, but even with the imitation of other artists, to such a degree, as in some measure to have brought about, in this country, a kind of revolution.' His furniture, however, was not intended for general production; it was designed for individual patrons and for particular settings.

To Hepplewhite must be given the credit for adapting Adam's new forms and ornament to the uses of cabinet-makers in general. The designs in the *Guide* (and those by Shearer in the *Book of Prices*) are at once elegant and practical. They follow 'the prevailing fashion only'.

Sheraton, on the other hand, despite a common debt to Adam and reliance on accepted formulae, drew on new fashions obtaining about 1790 (see below, pages 28–30). He aimed at novelty, choosing to give designs for those articles for which he felt able to make some original contribution. The Sheraton style is accomplished and studiedly elegant, and a refinement on that represented in the *Guide*. The *Drawing Book* illustrates the culminating phase of eighteenth-century furniture design — one which may be described as 'post-Hepplewhite'. It precedes the Regency (of which the foundations were laid during the period 1790–1800) and the break with eighteenth-century tradition.

THOMAS SHERATON (1751–1806)

Thomas Sheraton was born in Stockton-on-Tees, in the county of Durham, in 1751. Little is known of his family or of his first forty years of life and often the information we have is conjectural or drawn from his own published works. He was perhaps bred in poor circumstances: he describes himself, at the age of 31, as a workman — 'a mechanic, and one who never received the advantages of a *collegial* or *academical* education'. The phrase appears in the preface to a religious tract published at Stockton in 1782 by 'Thomas Sheraton Junr'. This work (to which was added *A Letter on the Subject of Baptism written to a Gentlewoman at her Request*) was entitled *A Scriptural Illustration of the Doctrine of Regeneration* . . . and expressed, says Sheraton, 'the honest sentiments of his heart'.[1] He may be believed then to have been employed as 'a journeyman cabinet-maker', working long hours, probably at Stockton, and his achievement was considerable. He possessed talents, not common to the artisan class, and much ability. He was a competent draughtsman, and two engraved views of Stockton High Street, after 'T. Sheraton', which were published about this time by a local bookseller and printer, are presumably from his hand (Plate 4). But he laboured, it would seem, under a sense of social inferiority.[2] There is no evidence as to where or by what means he acquired his education, and it is possible that the 'Gentlewoman in Norwich' at whose request he had composed the *Letter on the Subject of Baptism* gave him encouragement and help. He was, he states, 'connected in Church fellowship' with this lady 'for a short time', and the relationship existing between them may have been maintained by correspondence.

He was, it would seem certain, by this time of the company of the Baptists, who were early established as a small community in Stockton and nearby Marton.

---

[1] He asks, in the preface, to be read fairly, and fearing prejudice, 'the corroding worm at the bottom of all', enjoins his public 'entirely to forget . . . the mean author', anticipating that, by some, his doctrines will be judged harshly and, because they issue from 'the hand of a mechanic', be deemed to result from 'a mad and reveried brain'.

[2] 'Sheraton' is an uncommon name, and there can be little doubt that he belonged to a local family of good standing, whose members had long been established in Stockton and neighbourhood. One branch was possessed of lands in Elwick, near West Hartlepool. Yeomen farmers of the name are recorded as living at Higher Stotfold, Embleton and Sedgefield — all places within a few miles of Elwick.

19

Thomas Sheraton (1751–1806)

According to David Douglas, the Baptist historian, writing in 1846, the beginnings had been made at Marton, where a small chapel had been built in 1752, when certain persons residing in the village had been 'led to embrace Baptist principles'. This chapel was later 'occupied by the Baptists in Stockton'. In 1785 'there were five churches connected with the Baptist denomination in the North, namely, Hamsterley, Rowley, and Sunderland, in Durham; and Hexham and New-castle, in Northumberland; also Marton, in Yorkshire; together with its offshoot, Stockton, in Durham. The ministers were, Messrs. Whitfield, Fernie, and Ross. The churches in the west riding of Yorkshire and Lancashire were also increasing'.[1]

About 1790, Sheraton came to London and is said after 1793 there to have 'supported himself, a wife, and two children, by his exertions as an author'.[2] He is recorded as living at various addresses in the course of the next fifteen years: at 4 Hart Street, Grosvenor Square (1791); 41 Davies Street, Grosvenor Square (between 1793 and 1795); 106 Wardour Street, Soho (from 1795); and later, for some years until his death, at 8 Broad Street, Golden Square. It is highly improbable that he made furniture during his later years; nor is it generally thought that he was actively interested in the production of any one workshop.[3] His trade card (bearing the Wardour Street address) advertises that he taught 'Perspective, Architecture and Ornaments', made 'Designs for Cabinet-makers' and sold 'all kinds of Drawing Books' (Plate 96B). But it may be noted that he inscribes himself on the title page of the *Drawing Book* (his most important work, and one on which his reputation securely stands)[4] as 'Thomas Sheraton, Cabinet-Maker'.

In London, where there was a strong Baptist following,[5] Sheraton became a member of the Church in Little Prescot Street, Goodman's Fields, of which the Rev. Abraham Booth was minister. He was, at that time, a 'Scotch Baptist', then ordinary;[6] he had, that is, association with Churches which were Sandemanian or McLeanite in sympathy. (The term 'Scotch Baptist' had not then its present-day significance, since the only Baptists in Scotland were those generally called

---

[1] David Douglas, *History of the Baptist Churches in the North of England*, pp. 173, 224.

[2] Sheraton's obituary notice, which appeared in the *Gentleman's Magazine* for November 1806, under the heading of 'obituary, with Anecdotes, of remarkable Persons'. The names of his children are not recorded, but it is possible that a 'T. Sheraton', who exhibited paintings at the R.A. in the 1840's, was his son.

[3] An 'N. Sheraton' cabinet-maker of London, however, figures in the list of subscribers to the *Drawing Book*. A cabinet-maker of this name is likely to have been related to Sheraton.   [4] See below, pp. 25–32.

[5] In the *London Guide . . . published for J. Fielding*, 1782, it is stated that of the 315 different churches in London, including parish churches, 33 were for Baptists. Twenty 'Particular Baptist churches' are listed in the *Baptist Annual Register for 1794* (by John Rippon, D.D.).

[6] 'An Index to Notable Baptists', *Transactions of the Baptist Historical Society*, vii, 1920–1, p. 229.

McLeanists.) He continued to devote himself to questions of religion and in 1794 published a tract entitled *Scriptural Subjection to Civil Government* . . . issued in conjunction with *Thoughts on the Peaceable and Spiritual Nature of Christ's Kingdom* . . . by 'A Friend to Peace'. (The author of the latter, Adam Callander, a landscape painter then living in Titchfield Street, was an acquaintance and an associate in the Church.) And he put forward a scheme 'for evangelising the villages around London' by means of 'some form of open-air preaching, and gathering of children together for Christian teaching',[1] with, perhaps, some measure of success; but his efforts were short-lived. In about 1799 he left London and returned to the north.[2]

There occurred an event the following year which must have touched Sheraton deeply and, if foreseen by him, may have been the determining factor in his leaving London. He 'was called by the Church to assist . . . in the ministerial office'. When the Northern Baptist Association met at Rowley in 1800, 'Messrs. Valentine Short and Sheraton were ordained ministers of the small Baptist Church, meeting at Stockton-on-Tees, and Marton, Yorkshire. The former, Mr. Short', writes Douglas, reporting what had happened within living memory, 'had been connected with this church for many years, and had been its principal prop. On the demise of Mr. David Fernie, in the end of 1789, he was the chief individual who carried on worship, in the little community. He preached to the brethren, in his own house, at Stockton; and once a month administered the Lord's supper to them, at Marton.' Douglas continues: 'In 1799, Mr. Sheraton, a member of Mr. Abraham Booth's Church, London, and a distinguished mechanic, coming to reside in Darlington, was called by the Church to assist Mr. Short in the ministerial office. Messrs. Whitfield and Hassell conducted the services of the ordination. The meetings of the church had, for some time previously to this, been held in a long room of Mr. Sheraton's, and continued to be so, till his removal, and Mr. Short's death in 1802.'[3] The implied contradiction of the account is unexplained. Why, if the meetings of the brethren were held 'in a long room of Mr. Sheraton's, and continued to be so', is Sheraton said, without comment, to have come to reside in Darlington? It is conceivable that Sheraton journeyed to and from meetings at Stockton, but not that the brethren made their several ways to Darlington. Mr. Sheraton's 'long room' must surely have

[1] E. F. Kevan, *London's Oldest Baptist Church*, 1933, p. 102.
[2] For this and much other information concerning Sheraton's activities as a Baptist I am indebted to the Rev. Dr. E. A. Payne, General Secretary of the Baptist Union of Great Britain and Ireland.
[3] Douglas, op. cit., p. 242.

been in or by Stockton. It is possible that he had inherited money or property and had gained some necessary degree of independence. He and Valentine Short had been ordained together, with the laying on of hands, to the joint lay-pastorate of Marton and Stockton. His position in the community was that of lay-leader, but his way of life remains obscure. We know only that in 1801, when the Northern Baptist Association met at Hamsterley, he was one of the preachers. He left the district in 1802, and the church 'continued its meetings, in different parts of Stockton; occasionally enjoying the services of a minister, whose expenses they defrayed by making, according to apostolic direction, a contribution every Lord's day'.

The *Cabinet Dictionary* (with 'An Explanation of all the Terms used in the Cabinet, Chair & Upholstery Branches; with Directions for Varnish-making, Polishing, and Gilding. . . . The whole illustrated on Eighty-eight handsomely-engraved Copper-plates, including a very great Variety of the most fashionable Pieces of Cabinet Furniture . . .'), on which Sheraton afterwards was engaged, was published in 1803. The text is often verbose, though containing much useful and reliable information on the trade and contemporary methods of work; and the plates are of unequal merit. It is certainly a less successful work than the *Drawing Book*. Sheraton was perhaps out of sympathy with the stylistic trends of fashion in the early nineteenth century; and it is likely that his powers of invention were failing. 'Though', he writes at this time, 'I am thus employed in racking my invention to design fine and pleasing cabinet work, I can be well content to sit on a wooden bottom chair myself, provided I can but have common food and raiment wherewith to pass through life in peace.' There are indications that he was a weary and dispirited man.

In 1804, when occupied on his last work (*The Cabinet-Maker, Upholsterer, and General Artists' Encyclopædia*), he took into his home (in Broad Street, near Golden Square) Adam Black, the publisher, who was then a youth seeking employment in London. Black, in his *Memoirs*, recalls vividly their brief association: 'He lived in an obscure street, his house half shop, half dwelling-house, and looked himself like a worn-out Methodist minister, with threadbare black coat. I took tea with them one afternoon. There were a cup and saucer for the host, and another for his wife, and a little porringer for their daughter. The wife's cup and saucer were given to me, and she had to put up with another little porringer. My host seemed a good man, with some talent. He had been a cabinetmaker, was now author and publisher, teacher of drawing, and, I believe, occasional preacher. I was with him for about a week, engaged in most wretched work, writing a few articles, and trying to put his shop in order, working among dirt and bugs, for which I was remunerated with half a guinea. Miserable as the pay was, I was half ashamed to take it from the poor man.' *The Memoirs of Adam Black* was not published until 1885, some ten years after the subject's death. It was edited (and, in fact, written) by Alexander Nicolson from Black's autobiographical notes, compiled between 1864 and 1872. There is, however, no reason to question his accuracy: these few statements are confirmed in essentials by what is known about Sheraton from other sources. Black, at this time, and when away from home, habitually kept a diary, addressed to his parents. He says further of Sheraton in this diary: 'He is a man of talents, and, I believe, of genuine piety. He understands the cabinet business — I believe was bred to it; he has been, and perhaps at present is, a preacher; he is a scholar, writes well; draws, in my opinion, masterly; is an author, bookseller, stationer, and teacher. We may be ready to ask how comes it to pass that a man with such abilities and resources is in such a state? I believe his abilities and resources are his ruin, in this respect, for by attempting to do everything he does nothing.' Black's estimate of his employer was charitable, and his words kindly; but by 1804, Sheraton's mind had given way. He was then immersed in the *Encyclopædia*, an immense undertaking, only in part completed. ('30 numbers, in folio' were issued; and a single volume, covering A to C, was published in 1805.) Black contributed a few articles to the work, which is pretentious and often incoherent, bearing no relation to its title and which is illustrated with coloured plates of poor quality. He must have been aware of Sheraton's mental deterioration.

In 1805, too, there appeared a pamphlet, *The Character of God as Love*, a copy of which survives in the Brown Library, Providence, Rhode Island. This tract was published in Glasgow. There is therefore the suggestion of continued association with the 'Scotch Baptists'.

We learn from Sheraton's obituary notice in the *Gentleman's Magazine* that 'in order to increase the number of his subscribers to this work [the *Encyclopædia*], he had lately visited Ireland, where he obtained the sanction of the Lord Lieutenant, the Marchioness of Donegal, and other distinguished persons'. Whether or not this represented his normal practice is open to question. He may, in former years, have found it expedient to travel, seeking subscribers to his works, in the provinces. He may have been able to combine this with other business, bringing news of improvements in the metropolis to the country. 'He was', continues the notice, 'a very honest, well-disposed man; of an acute and enterprising disposition. . . .'

He died on 22 October 1806, 'in Broad-street, Soho, after a few days illness of a phrenitis, aged 55', and left his family 'in distressed circumstances'.[1]

A posthumous work, entitled *Designs for Household Furniture, by the late T. Sheraton, cabinet maker*, was published in 1812 by J. Taylor 'at the Architectural Library, 59 High Holborn'. It contained patterns 'in the Cabinet, Chair, and Upholsterery Branches on Eighty-four plates', taken from Sheraton's books, previously published.

[1] He was buried on the 27th (Parish Register of St. James's Church, Piccadilly). The following month, Letters of Administration were granted to his widow, Margaret Sheraton; £200 (Wills Registry, Somerset House).

It is of interest that in the same year, also in London, there died (at Featherstone Buildings) one, Robert Sheraton, 'gentleman, formerly of Stockton'. He had owned lands at Elwick. (Will in Durham District Registry.)

'THE DRAWING BOOK'

The Cabinet-Maker and Upholsterer's Drawing-Book, in three parts, with the *Appendix* . . . and *An Accompaniment to the . . . Drawing-Book*, was issued in 49 separate numbers between 1791 and 1794.

The several parts of the work are of unequal value. Parts I and II are devoted respectively to lengthy dissertations on geometry and perspective; they permit Sheraton to parade his knowledge of these subjects, and are unlikely to have been of much practical use to his readers (Sheraton, it should be remembered, advertised that he *taught* 'Perspective, Architecture and Ornaments'.) They throw light on Sheraton's ambitious, uneasy mentality. 'No workman need to be shocked', he observes in his introduction, 'or frightened at the idea of learning such geometrical lines and figures as shall be considered in the subsequent pages.' He claims of perspective that its value to 'Cabinet-makers, Upholsterers, Chairmakers, Joiners, and other persons concerned with designing, cannot be disputed on good grounds'. A master 'cannot possibly convey to the workmen', he states, 'so just an idea of a piece of furniture by a verbal description, as may be done by a good sketch, proportioned according to the laws of perspective. . . .' He is at pains to provide assistance for the unlearned 'in the derivation of particular words used in Geometry, Architecture, and Perspective, in order to fix', so he says, 'their real meaning more lastingly' on the mind; and numerous derivations from the Greek, abstracted from contemporary standard sources, are appended as footnotes. Sheraton's continued efforts to acquire learning and, in particular, his interest in Greek, which appears also in the *Cabinet Dictionary* and the *Encyclopædia*, bear perhaps on his preoccupation with theological matters, early evinced by the tract, the *Doctrine of Regeneration*, and by his activities as an occasional preacher among Baptists.

Part III, on the other hand, is practical and informative. Sheraton here proposes 'to exhibit the present taste of furniture, and at the same time to give the workman some assistance . . .'; and in these aims he is entirely successful. The descriptions of furniture illustrated in the plates, and his observations 'on the manufacturing part of such pieces', their 'use and style of finishing', exceed those contained in earlier pattern books. He possessed a good technical knowledge of the cabinet trade and was fully conversant with recent improvements adopted in the London workshops. The *Drawing Book* is, moreover, exceptional in as much as it was written by 'a journeyman cabinet-maker', then living 'by his exertions as an author'. Sheraton had no need 'to keep knowledge to himself, as his own property, and upon which his bread may depend', and although apprehensive that his book would not 'meet with the approbation of those who wished to hoard up their own knowledge to themselves, lest any should share in the advantage arising from it', he saw no 'impropriety in persons of the same branch informing each other. In trades where their arts depend on secrets', he continues, 'it is right for men to keep them from strangers; but the art of cabinet-making depends so much on practice, and requires so many tools, that a stranger cannot steal it.'

The *Appendix* and *An Accompaniment*, published separately and subsequently, are sections which may be regarded as complementary to Part III and are therefore of importance. The former, which gave 'a variety of original designs for household furniture, in the newest and most elegant style, and, also, a number of plain and useful pieces, suitable either for town or country, together with a description and explanation to each piece', was issued in 1793; the latter, consisting of 'ornaments useful for learners to copy from, but particularly adapted to the cabinet and chair branches: exhibiting original and new designs of chair legs, bed pillars, window cornices, chair splads and other ornaments . . .', in 1794.[1]

The designs for furniture shown in these plates are excellent, both as regards draughtsmanship and invention. Many are in themselves pleasing minor works of art. Sheraton was an accomplished artist, with a definite and individual style. If we are to believe the young Adam Black, he drew 'masterly'. His line is clean and explanatory; he is able successfully to render texture and ornament, to shadow and make use of cast shadows without obscuring details of construction — and he was versed in the intricacies of his subject matter.

The extent to which he was directly responsible for their invention is uncertain. There are indications that he had a large acquaintance among masters and workmen

[1] Of the 113 plates contained in the complete *Drawing Book*, 27 relate to Parts I and II (frontispiece, 1–13 and 14–26), 39 to Part III (25–61, plus 29A and 56A), 33 to the *Appendix* (1–32, plus 30A) and 14 to the *Accompaniment*. (Five plate numbers, as indicated, are duplicated.) Plates illustrating the treatises on geometry and perspective are much in the minority. The second edition of the *Drawing Book*, which appeared in 1794, was enlarged by 8 additional new plates. These figure in the *Appendix*, which was perhaps the most useful section of the work. It may be significant that copies of the *Appendix* dated 1796 exist. The third edition, in four parts, was published in 1802 and contains 122 plates. (Part IV here comprises the *Appendix* and the *Accompaniment*.) The additions to text and plates are inconsiderable.

in the London shops, and perhaps in the provinces. 'In conversing with cabinet-makers', he says, 'I find no one individual equally experienced in every job of work. There are certain pieces made in one shop which are not manufactured in another. . . . For this reason I have made it my business to apply to the best work-men in different shops, to obtain their assistance in the explanation of such pieces as they have been most acquainted with. And, in general, my request has been complied with. . . .' He relied, therefore, not only on his own 'knowledge and experience . . . of the business' but on 'that of other good workmen'. There is evidence that some designs had already been executed before publication of the *Drawing Book*. Sheraton's assurance that his text might 'be depended on by those who have not yet had an opportunity of seeing the different pieces executed', although of limited application, would seem to be significant in this connection. And, in one form or another, he specifically acknowledges indebtedness to in-dividuals: an oval library table, similar to that illustrated in Plate XXX, had, he observes, been supplied to the Duke of York (Plate 39); 'the first idea' of the 'Summer-Bed in two Compartments' (Plate XLI) was 'communicated' to him 'by Mr. Thompson, groom of the household furniture to the Duke of York'; and of the 'Harlequin Pembroke Table' (Plate LVI) he writes: 'I assume very little originality or merit to myself, except what is due to the manner of shewing and describing the mechanism of it: the rest is due to a friend, from whom I received my first ideas.' Again, his remarks on knife cases, shown in Plate XXXIX, are of interest: 'As these cases are not made in regular cabinet shops, it may be of ser-vice to mention where they are executed in the best taste, by one who makes it his main business; *i.e.* John Lane, No. 44, St. Martin's-le-grand, London.' Proof of prior execution of a design would not necessarily preclude its having been originally his conception.

Sheraton advertised later his readiness to supply designs to cabinet-makers (Plate 96B), and there is no reason to doubt, in view of his abilities, that he was actively employed in this way. He received one such commission, at least, from John Broadwood, providing the design for an historic grand piano, with a com-pass of six octaves, constructed by the firm in 1796 for Don Manuel de Godoy, Prince of the Peace, and presented by him to Queen Maria Louisa of Spain.[1] But, in general, we do not know for whom he worked, his range or volume of business;

[1] The instrument, in a satinwood case, banded with mahogany and inset with Wedgwood's and Tassie's medallions, took four months to make and cost 213 guineas, exclusive of extra charges, mainly for pack-ing. Formerly the property of the first Viscount Leverhulme, it was sold in New York in 1926.

and his original drawings, with perhaps one exception, are not known to have survived (Plate 3).

The 'present taste of furniture', exhibited in the *Drawing Book*, is new. Sheraton's designs differ in style, often quite considerably, from those published by Hepplewhite and Shearer in the *Guide* and the *Book of Prices* (although the latter may be taken substantially to reflect current production) and make a distinct advance on them. The style with which his name is rightly to be associated (and which is expressed in these earlier designs) is individual and remarkably consistent, having affinities with that existing in France in the later years of the reign of Louis XVI and maintained under the *Directoire*. His designs are usually elaborate and often extremely ornamental, but the forms employed, by contrast, are simple and severe. Sheraton, although disclaiming admiration for French workmanship, possessed an awareness of French fashions that was uncommon at this particular time.[1] A considerable quantity of Louis XVI furniture, brought into England by the first *émigrés*, had already appeared on the London market by about 1790 or 1791, when Sheraton was working on the *Drawing Book*. He may have had an opportunity of studying some of this furniture. He may also have had contact with French craftsmen who took refuge in this country from the Revolution. He was certainly indebted to French models for such articles of furniture as the 'conversation chair' and the 'duchesse' (see pages 53–54).

The designs exhibit various distinctive features. Some represent a logical development of those to be found in the *Guide*; others are new, and some were in turn developed in the nineteenth century. Sheraton, like Hepplewhite, makes use of both the slender taper leg of square section and the turned cylindrical leg, but shows an increased dependence on the latter form, particularly for drawing room chairs, pier tables and the more ornamental of his cabinets. He prefers reeding to fluting as a decoration on the legs and front surfaces of his furniture. Reeding was the later and more fashionable feature, and often concomitant with the turned leg. The brass handles on his (as on Hepplewhite's) cabinets, tables and chests-of-drawers are usually circular in shape, ornamented or plain, whether in the form of a plate with ring handle, a small knob or a ring. He, like Hepplewhite, freely adopts ornamental *motifs* often derived from Adam, such as the urn, the vase, swags, *paterae*, bouquets and garlands of flowers, the ribbon and the

---

[1] 'The quality of cabinet work is extremely variable in both countries, arising chiefly from the abilities of the workman, the directions given him, or the state of the wood which is used to work on. . . .' Were it not for the excellence of French brass mounts, 'by which they set off cabinet work', states Sheraton in the *Cabinet Dictionary*, it would not 'bear a comparison with ours, neither in design, nor neatness of execution'.

plume. His arabesque ornament is extremely intricate. His treatment of acanthus, springing from elaborately curved and 'spiky' stems, and of anthemion, has a quality of brittleness that is not present in Hepplewhite. He relies also on an ornament of inlaid stringing lines, used in conjunction with contrasting veneers, laid in geometrical patterns (often oval or lozenge-shaped) on large flat or gently curving surfaces, as the doors of wardrobes or the fronts of chests-of-drawers (Plate 91). Sheraton had a highly developed sense of proportion and balance but his designs, perhaps, are occasionally over-refined. The effeminate character of some is emphasized by his liberal employment of draperies and by an interest in an elaborated upholstery (Plate 12). Such designs as those for a cabinet, with silk and festoons of drapery in the centre door (Plate 70), for beds and *chaises longues* have no counterpart in the *Guide*. His use of brass, a new feature, for which he was indebted to French models and of which mention has already been made (footnote, page 28) is noteworthy. Brass enrichments appear in the form of small galleries or of strings (Plate 39) and brass rods are provided as a useful fitting for sideboards (Plate 42). Sheraton is more versatile than Hepplewhite. A willingness to experiment is apparent in a design for a Pembroke table supported on 'pillar and claws' (an unusual form anticipating one variety of sofa table), and designs for a 'Horse Dressing Glass & Writing Table' (Plate 83), as in the oval writing table (Plate 39) and 'kidney table' (Plate 44). For some writing tables and work tables he introduces lyre-shaped end supports, or standards, on splayed feet — a form which was to enjoy great popularity. Pier tables and the stands of ladies' cabinets are shown often with stretchers uniting in a shelf, or a low platform, with a considerable gain in decorative effect. His skill and inventiveness as a designer, instanced by a plate giving patterns for 'Pediments for Bookcases' (Plate 25), is particularly marked when he is dealing with new forms.

He was, certainly, influenced by Henry Holland, whose work he much admired, and indebted to him for some elements of his style. Holland, in his capacity as architect to the Prince of Wales, had been actively engaged since 1783 on the redecoration and refurnishing of Carlton House. Furniture, supplied by leading firms, was made under his direction and often to his designs. The interior of Carlton House was seen by Sheraton in 1793, when he was occupied with the production of later numbers of the *Drawing Book*, and he was sufficiently impressed by the decorations to make drawings of two of the rooms — the 'Chinese Drawing Room' and the 'Dining Room' (Plates 27, 96A). These he subsequently published, with descriptions, in the *Drawing Book* and *Appendix*. The 'Plan & Section of a Drawing Room', an elaborate plate showing the elevations of each of the four walls of the room, was inspired too by Holland (Plate 26). He was, it has been said, 'the champion and exponent of the straight line in furniture making'.[1] The *elevations* of his designs, therefore, are usually rigidly rectangular. Unlike Adam (and Hepplewhite), but following the example of Holland, he makes little use of shield, oval or circular shapes, even for chairs, sofas and mirrors. Such designs as those for tripod and horse fire screens or candle stands are exceptional. The severity of his forms is modified occasionally by the introduction of a dome (as, for example, in the design for 'An Eliptic Bed for a Single Lady') or the various segmental pediments suggested for bookcases and other case furniture; and it is relieved by painted and inlaid arabesque ornament.[2] On the other hand, the system adopted in the *plans* of the designs is curvilinear. He experiments with contrasting convex and concave outlines, with recesses and rounded projections (Plate 73). He tends also to stress the vertical components of a design, often by the use of engaged colonnettes or pilasters, which are extended and given prominence so as to interrupt all mouldings (Colour Plate D and Plate 70); similarly, the legs of tables and chairs are continued upwards at their junction with frieze or seat rail, and projecting, break the horizontal lines of these parts (Plate 12).

The balance of probability, on stylistic grounds, is that full credit is due to him for the invention or development of the majority, at least, of the *Drawing Book* designs. It would seem unlikely that they are copies taken from finished work in the shops of fashionable cabinet makers of his acquaintance. His own reference to those of his subscribers who 'say many of the designs are rather calculated to shew what may be done, than to exhibit what is or has been done in the trade' confirms this view.

More than 700 individuals are listed as subscribers to the first edition of the *Drawing Book*. They were, with few exceptions, tradesmen. Cabinet-makers and upholsterers account for a very large proportion of the total; and various joiners, carvers and gilders, chair-makers and makers of musical instruments, with book-sellers and printers who had reason to be interested in the work, also subscribed. We find, too, several of the different engravers employed by Sheraton to work on the plates and persons commissioned in allied trades, such as plasterers, 'mahogany-

---

[1] H. D. Eberlein and A. McClure, *The Practical Book of Period Furniture*, Philadelphia, 1914.
[2] He favours oval shapes in his patterns for the glazing bars of bookcase doors, and oval 'panelling' on flat surfaces.

merchants' and plane-makers; and painters, 'profile painters' and drawing masters, amongst whom Sheraton may be presumed to have had some acquaintance. The number of private individuals whose names occur is negligible, perhaps because Sheraton, who was not a working cabinet-maker, had no clientele, except within the trade. (Hepplewhite, by contrast, had proposed that the *Guide* should be 'useful to the mechanic and serviceable to the gentleman'.)

About 450 subscribers to the *Drawing Book* lived or had businesses in London, and about 200 in the provinces. These latter were drawn largely from the north-east, from the counties of Yorkshire, Northumberland and Durham (and from Lincolnshire), and from the newer industrial towns of Newcastle (21), Sheffield (18), Leeds (16) and Halifax (8). There are indications that Sheraton had not severed ties with Stockton (7), and the area of his birth. He may, perhaps, be believed to have had associations with Norwich (11) and Ipswich (10), although conjecturally (see pages 19, 81); and, possibly, about 1790, to have visited Scotland, since subscribers there number more than 40, whereas both Wales and Ireland are unrepresented (see page 23). The distribution of subscribers throughout the country as a whole is noticeably uneven, being relatively thin in the Home Counties, the west and north-west; and Sheraton may be supposed, to a degree that is uncertain, to have been in touch with subscribers, either in person or by proxy.

Sheraton's influence, through the *Drawing Book*, on the design of furniture in the last decade of the century, particularly in London, must have been very considerable, if often of an indirect nature. That is not to say that the designs characterize the general style of furniture made in these years. Makers who subscribed to the *Drawing Book* did so because they believed it to their advantage to possess a ready source of information on new fashions. Even if influenced by the designs, or by Sheraton's ideas, they were not dependent on them, doubtless preferring to develop their own stock-in-trade and to improve on patterns that were established in their workshops. Cabinet-making was a traditional craft, and furniture of this period exhibits for the most part a marked continuity of style. Much of it, whether made in town or country, was of a plain and serviceable nature, designed with small regard to fashion. The over-all stylistic development of furniture in the late eighteenth century cannot be precisely charted. Many pieces exhibit features (in a variable degree) that may be associated specifically with Sheraton — or with Hepplewhite, or both designers; but such features persist and are also to be found in work of the early nineteenth century.

There is also the problem of 'continuing production'. Certain designs (or features of them), whether by Sheraton or others, were reproduced, for differing reasons, long after they had ceased to be 'the newest fashion' (see page 65). As has been remarked, 'continuing production' is a type of time-lag: 'It was necessary long before to-day — indeed the contrary would be unnatural — to make good the hazards of use. . . . The neglected talents of the estate carpenter were of course constantly invoked. But any country cousin coming to London could be sure, as bills and reason alike remind one, of replacement in the shops. There were diehard tastes, and house conventions, as well as mere damage.'[1]

Finally, some count should be taken of the production of well-known firms such as Wright & Mansfield or Johnstone & Jeanes, who, working from the middle of the nineteenth century, adapted the style of Sheraton to suit contemporary requirements. 'Reproductions' of this nature were not made with intention to deceive, and material indication of their date of origin, in one form or another, is rarely absent. The workmanship was usually of a very high quality.

[1] W. A. Thorpe, 'Walpole and after', in *Country Life*, 12 January 1951.

C. Side table, of painted pine wood; Irish, c. 1790.
Victoria and Albert Museum.

SOME CONTEMPORARY MAKERS

SEDDON'S

At this period, Seddon's was of first importance. George Seddon, the founder of the firm, had set up in the trade in London about 1750. He became a liveryman of the Joiners' Company and, by 1768, when his premises in Aldersgate Street were destroyed by fire, was judged 'one of the most eminent cabinet-makers of London'. He had then, according to a newspaper report, eighty cabinet-makers in his employ. He continued to prosper (at London House, Aldersgate Street) and his stock-in-trade, by December 1789, was valued at nearly £119,000 — timber alone amounting to more than £20,000. In the 1790's, the firm was styled 'Seddon, Sons and Shackleton' (George and Thomas, Seddon's sons, and his son-in-law Thomas Shackleton, having been taken into partnership).

A detailed, contemporary account of the workshops, which were very extensive, survives in the diary of Sophie von la Roche.[1] This lady, a German novelist and traveller, visited the establishment in September 1786. She tells us that Seddon employed four hundred journeymen 'on any work connected with the making of household furniture'. The craftsmen (joiners, carvers, upholsterers, gilders, workers in ormolu, mirror-workers and locksmiths) were 'housed in a building with six wings'. Plate glass for mirrors was cast and cut in the basement. The saw-house, 'where as many blocks of fine foreign wood lie piled, as firs and oaks are seen at our saw-mills', she finds of particular interest: 'The entire story of the wood', she remarks, 'as used for both inexpensive and costly furniture and the method of treating it, can be traced in this establishment.'

There were 'chintz, silk and wool materials for curtains and bed-covers; hangings in every possible material; carpets and stair-carpets to order; in short, anything one might desire to furnish a house' — and 'a great many seamstresses'.

Seddon, she believes to be able and benevolent: 'Seddon, foster-father to four hundred employees, seemed to me a respectable man, a man of genius, too, with

[1] *Sophie in London, 1786*, trans. from the German by Clare Williams, 1933, pp. 173–5

an understanding for the needs of the needy and the luxurious . . . intimate with the quality of woods from all parts of the earth.' She alludes to his being 'for ever creating new forms'. The phrase suggests strongly that an appreciable amount of furniture was executed from original designs by Seddon, or from those of designers employed by him. We know that, at London House, finished articles of furniture were stocked 'in all manner of wood and patterns, from the simplest and cheapest to the most elegant and expensive'. It is reasonable to assume that a fair proportion of this stock was of distinctive character (Colour Plate B).

Branches of the business existed, in the 1790's, at 10 Charterhouse Street and at 24 Dover Street, in the charge of Thomas Seddon (a subscriber, incidentally, to the *Drawing Book*). They carried, perhaps, a more specialized stock.

GILLOW'S

Gillow's, like Seddon's, was a family business of importance, established through several generations. Gillow's, however, was not, primarily, a London firm. The founder, Robert Gillow, a native of the parish of Kirkham-in-the-Fylde, is stated to have settled, about 1695, in Lancaster, working as a carpenter. He was made a freeman of the borough in 1728 and entered the ranks of local cabinet-makers.

The records of the firm survive from 1731. About 1757, Richard (1734–1811), the eldest son of Robert Gillow (1703–73), was taken into partnership; subsequently, his brothers, Robert and Thomas, joined the business. There is evidence, thenceforward, of the Gillows' many enterprises. They, like other merchants of Lancaster (then a principal seaport, second only to Bristol), traded with the West Indies, exporting furniture and taking timber, sugar, cotton and rum in payment. (The Gillows were 'Licensed Dealers in Rum'.) Their export trade was on a considerable scale and it is said that the shops 'received from the workmen by whom they were occupied designations after the names of places to which consignments were made, such as Barbadoes, St. Domingo, St. Helena, Cape of Good Hope, and New Britain'.[1] They were active in various building and surveying works, notably for public buildings in Lancaster between 1758 and 1790. (The Old Custom House, a handsome porticoed Palladian building of the Ionic order, with rusticated base, was designed by Richard Gillow in 1764.)

[1] *Gillow's: A Record of a furnishing firm During Two Centuries*, London, 1901.

34

Their cabinet trade, in the latter part of the century, was very extensive. Thomas Pennant, in his *Tour in Scotland*, refers to Lancaster, in passing, as being 'famous in having some very ingenious cabinet-makers . . . who fabricate most excellent and neat goods at remarkably cheap rates, which they export to London and the plantations'. The allusion to the London trade (described in the Gillow books under the heading 'Adventure to London') is interesting, particularly in view of the date at which he was writing (1772): Gillow's would seem first to have sent furniture to London for sale about 1740. This early venture was successful, apparently, and maintained; and its continuance is in some measure proof of the quality of their goods. Consignments were sent by sea from Lancaster, the coastal voyage (providing cheap and reasonably secure transport) taking between ten and fourteen days. For many years, the shipments were warehoused. In, or before, 1771, however, their volume of trade was sufficiently large to merit the opening of a London branch, under the management of Robert junior (d. 1796) and Taylor, a partner. (The entry 'Gillow and Taylor, Cabinet-makers and Upholsterers, 176, Oxford Road' is contained in Kent's directory for 1771.) The site chosen was in a new and fashionable quarter of the town, and doubtless the premises served as showrooms, stocking furniture made in Lancaster. About 1776, Robert Gillow settled in London, and from 1779 (after the death of Taylor), the firm was styled 'Robert, Richard and Thomas Gillow'. Later, from 1790 to 1803, it became 'Robert Gillow and Co.'.

Gillow's enjoyed a good clientele and obtained substantial commissions. Messrs. Robins, a Covent Garden firm of auctioneers, who, about 1797, sold the effects of 'A Man of Fashion, At his House, No. 24 Piccadilly' advertise the 'very excellent Cabinet Furniture of every description, by that excellent maker, Mr. Gillow, of Oxford Street'.

The firm's dispute with Mrs. Piozzi is well known, and was disadvantageous to both parties. Mrs. Piozzi, who was concerned after her marriage in 1794 to refurnish Streatham Park 'in modern style, supremely elegant', selected Gillow's for the work — as having, presumably, the reputation for being 'not expensive', and as being a firm of high standing. She received goods from Gillow's to the value of £2,380, was advised that the charges were excessive and, eventually, settled for £2,070.

In general, Gillow's charges are known to have been very moderate. Among the firm's records at Lancaster (in the possession of Messrs. Waring & Gillow, Ltd., Lancaster) is a series of 'E.S. books', or cost books, some dating from the late eighteenth century. These books contain estimates and rough sketches of the furniture made, entered by the clerk entrusted with their keeping, and provide much invaluable information as to details of output (Plates 18, 19, 58, 59, 78–81, 92, 93). Gillow's, as might be expected, had many clients from the north. Their work was often surprisingly conservative in design, and of simple, useful character.

Gillow's are described by a German visitor in 1807 as 'the first grade salesmen and manufacturers in London; they deal widely in land and foreign trade and maintain employees in different parts of England; their work is good and solid, though not of the first class in inventiveness and style'.[1] This judgement may be accepted (Plate 61).

JOHN McLEAN AND SON

McLean is included by Sheraton in his 'List of most of the Master Cabinet-makers, Upholsterers, and Chair Makers, in and about London, for 1803', which is appended to the *Cabinet Dictionary*. 'M'Lean and Son', upholsterers and cabinet-makers, were at the Upper Terrace, Tottenham Court Road, and Marylebone Street. According to their trade card (in the Banks collection at the British Museum), they later specialized in 'Elegant Parisian Furniture'. The first of two designs for 'Pouch Tables', Plate 65 in the *Cabinet Dictionary*, is stated by Sheraton to have been 'taken from one executed by Mr. M'Lean in Mary-le-bone street, near Tottenham court road, who finishes these small articles in the neatest manner'. It is not improbable that Sheraton had business dealings with the firm. Furniture bearing McLean's label has survived. There is no doubt that the business was very substantial.

OAKLEY'S

'Oakley, Shackleton and Evans', with premises at 22 St. Paul's Churchyard and 8 Old Bond Street, figure as 'Upholsterers' in the *Cabinet Dictionary*. The senior partner of the firm was George Oakley, first recorded in the directories in 1790, and a subscriber to the *Drawing Book*. He had, at St. Paul's Churchyard, a

[1] P. A. Nemmich, *Neueste Reise durch England*, 1807.

36

'Magazine of General and superb upholstery and cabinet furniture'. Shackleton, who joined him about 1800, was formerly a partner in Seddon's.

'Oakeleys', in 1801, is referred to as being 'the most tasteful of the London cabinet-makers'.[1]

FRANCE AND BECKWITH

France and Beckwith, 'Upholsterers and Cabinet makers to His Majesty' were in partnership at 101 St. Martin's Lane. The firm had been established for many years at this address (and had been employed by the first Lord Mansfield at Kenwood between 1768 and 1770). The name occurs frequently in the Royal Household Accounts. 'France, St. Martin's-lane, Cabinet-maker to his Majesty' is listed among the subscribers to the *Drawing Book*.

ELLIOTT AND CO.

Sheraton, in the *Drawing Book*, names Charles Elliott 'Upholsterer to his Majesty, and Cabinet-maker to the Duke of York'. Best known of an old cabinet-making family, Elliott rivalled France in reputation. His name appears in the Royal Household Accounts from about 1784 (when Charles Elliott and Co. succeeded Davis and Elliott at 97 New Bond Street) until early in the nineteenth century. Nemmich,[2] in 1807, refers to 'Elliott & Co. and France' as 'the Royal upholsterers', and adds: 'These two firms, together with the undertakers, made arrangements for Nelson's funeral.'

ELWARD, MARSH AND CO.

This firm, variously styled in the late eighteenth and early nineteenth centuries, was established at 13 Mount Street. (William Marsh, 'upholder and cabinet-maker', is recorded at this address as early as 1778.) From 1795, Marsh and his partners were principal cabinet-makers to George, Prince of Wales and supplied furniture for Carlton House and Brighton Pavilion (Plate 17). The firm was joined

[1] The London correspondent of the *Journal des Luxus und der Moden* (Weimar).   [2] Op. cit.

by Thomas Tatham, elder brother of the architect, Charles Heathcote Tatham (1772–1842). The latter, a pupil of Henry Holland (1746–1806), exerted a considerable influence on furniture design and may also have been closely associated with the firm. Marsh and Tatham were employed at Southill, Bedfordshire, and received very substantial payments in 1801 and 1802. Thomas Tatham, who became head of the firm in 1809, died worth £60,000.

THOMAS CHIPPENDALE, THE YOUNGER (1749–1822)

After his father's death in 1779, the younger Chippendale continued the business at 60 St. Martin's Lane, trading as 'Chippendale and Haig'. The firm's standing was high, and it is significant that Chippendale was consulted (as were Ince and Mayhew, q.v.) by the Commissioners for the Prince of Wales's debts (1795) in connection with the claims of certain makers for furniture supplied for Carlton House. Chippendale was made bankrupt in 1804 (Haig having withdrawn some years previously) and his stock, which included 'many articles of great taste and of the finest workmanship', was sold by auction on the premises. The following year, however, he was again in business at the same address and described as 'upholsterer and cabinet maker to the Duke of Gloucester'. Chippendale supplied furniture for Wilton, Harewood House (1796–7) and Stourhead (1795–1820). He was a painter (exhibiting at the Royal Academy between 1784 and 1801) and an able designer and draughtsman. He is referred to by George Smith (*The Cabinet-maker and Upholsterer's Guide*, 1826) 'as possessing a very great degree of taste'.

INCE AND MAYHEW

William Ince and John Mayhew are now best known as the authors of the *Universal System of Household Furniture*, a large book of designs published in parts between 1759 and 1763. This work, which Sheraton refers to as 'Ince's book' and as being 'of merit in its day, though inferior to Chippendale's, which was a real original . . .', was produced in rivalry with the *Director* and was, in addition, aimed at the French market. The partners, who married two sisters (both at St. James's Church, Piccadilly, on 20 February 1762), had removed, by Sheraton's day, from premises at Broad Street, Soho, to Marshall Street, Carnaby Market, nearby; they are listed as 'Upholsterers' in the *Cabinet Dictionary*, 1803.

The firm supplied a large set of chairs to the Board of the Westminster Fire Office in 1792,[1] and furniture, in 1802, for Mrs. Piozzi's 'pretty Brynbella', near Flint.

Mayhew, who survived his partner, died in 1811.

Other makers whose names occur in the Lord Chamberlain's Accounts at this time for furniture supplied to the King were: *Richard Taitt*, upholsterer and joiner, of Jermyn Street (between 1793 and 1795); *John Taitt*, cabinet-maker and upholsterer, of Oxford Street (between 1793 and 1796); *John Russell*, chair-maker, upholsterer and cabinet-maker, of New Bond Street and (from 1793) of Broker Row, Moorfields (between 1773 and 1810); *William Adair*, carver and gilder, of Wardour Street, Soho (between 1799 and 1805).[2]

Among the tradesmen employed by the Prince of Wales at Carlton House between 1783 and 1795 under the direction of Henry Holland, the Prince's architect, were also: *Robert Campbell*, upholsterer and cabinet-maker, of Marylebone Street, Golden Square; *John West*, joiner and cabinet-maker, of Tufton Street, Westminster; *Francis Hervé*, 'French chair maker', of Lower John Street, Tottenham Court Road (Plate 36); *S. Nelson*, carver and gilder, of Marshall Street, Golden Square; *Ravald and Morland*, upholsterers, of Princes Street, Soho; *Nicholas Morel*, upholsterer, of Tenterden Street, Hanover Square (subsequently of Great Marlborough Street). The Prince's chief cabinet-maker at this period was Campbell, trading as 'Campbell and Son'. His 'Estimate for Works' at Carlton House, submitted in 1789, amounted to £10,500. From 1795, his place was taken by 'Marsh and Tatham'.[3] Sheraton makes particular mention of Campbell in the *Drawing Book* and was indebted to him for his designs for library steps (see page 79).

[1] The chairs, which are still in use, are described and reproduced by C. Hussey in *Country Life*, 21 December 1951. The Office's badge, the portcullis and Prince of Wales's feathers, is incorporated in the design of the backs.

[2] See H. Clifford Smith, *Buckingham Palace*, 1931. [3] H. Clifford Smith, op. cit.

WOODS AND DECORATIVE PROCESSES

The London cabinet-makers had at their disposal numerous fine woods, many of which were used only for decorative inlays or bandings. Most of these woods were imported, often at considerable expense. According to William Marshall's *On Planting and Rural Ornament*, first published, 1785, *mahogany* and *beech* were chiefly in demand; 'next to these', he observes, 'follow *Dutch Oak* (Wainscot), *Deal*, *Elm*; and lastly *Walnuttree*, *Cherrytree*, *Plumtree*, *Box*, *Holly*, *Yew*, and a variety of woods for inlaying of cabinets. In some country places, a considerable quantity of *English Oak* is worked up into tables, chairs, drawers, and bedsteads; but, in London, *Beech* is almost the only English wood made use of, *at present*, by the cabinet and chair makers.'[1] Marshall's list is by no means comprehensive (and the omission of satinwood, in particular, is misleading). His argument relates to the employment of foreign woods to the exclusion of those of native growth.

A reliable indication of the stock of woods held at this time by a fashionable cabinet-maker is furnished by the notices of the younger Chippendale's bankruptcy sale. The sale of timber occupied three days and comprised 'very valuable old Jamaica, Spanish, Cuba and Honduras mahogany in plank and boards;[2] choice Satin, Rose and Kingswood, Cedar in logs, Walnut-tree, American Birch; and a selection of the most beautiful veneers of extraordinary dimensions and very scarce'.[3]

MAHOGANY

Mahogany, as in past years, was used extensively by cabinet-makers, both in the solid and as a figured veneer, more generally for dining room, library and bedroom furniture. The wood was imported from the Spanish islands of San Domingo

---

[1] 3rd ed., 1803, vol. I, pp. 51–2.
[2] 'Wood cut into inch and quarter, and all above, is called plank wood'.
[3] W. T. Whitley, *Artists and their friends in England, 1700–1799*, 1928, vol. II, pp. 262–3.

and Cuba, from Jamaica (a British possession) and Honduras. (The several varieties were often described generically, in the third quarter of the century, as 'Jamaica wood', as a consequence of the Spanish woods being shipped via Jamaica in evasion of duties then levied on foreign timbers.) The value of these imports in the 1790's was annually in the neighbourhood of £75,000 — a sum, more than double that obtaining in the mid-century, representing a very considerable tonnage. This heavy employment of an expensive wood was a matter for surprise to foreigners. 'It is indeed remarkable', writes a French visitor in 1784, 'that the English are so much given to the use of mahogany; not only are their tables generally made of it, but also their doors and seats and the handrails of their staircases. Yet it is just as dear in England as in France. . . . At all events, their tables are made of most beautiful wood and always have a brilliant polish like that of the finest glass.'[1]

The mahogany produced in San Domingo (Hispaniola) was commonly termed 'Spanish wood'.[2] Close-textured, heavy and extremely hard, and dark in colour (turning almost black with age), it took a natural polish. Much fine furniture of the early Chippendale period was made of the San Domingo mahogany. It was an excellent medium for the carver, and, 'in its vigour, crispness and finish often reminiscent of chased bronze'.[3] It possessed, however, little figure; and soon after 1750, with the readoption of veneered constructions and the decline of carving as an essential means of ornamentation, was less in demand — although, as late as 1775, Gillow's, a firm experienced in such importations, wrote to their agents abroad requesting 'Spanish wood from Hispaniola' as being 'the safest sort of mahogany to turn out good'.[4]

Cuban mahogany (or 'Havannah wood'), less hard, with a straight grain and of a rich, reddish-brown colour, was in favour after 1750 for furniture of high quality. Some cuts and growths, such as the decorative 'fiddle mottle' and 'curl', were specially valuable for their veneers. None the less, by the end of the century, it in turn was replaced in popularity by Honduras mahogany, obtained from coastal forests in that part of central America.

This latter, sometimes known as 'baywood' ('from the bay or arm of the sea

---

[1] *A Frenchman in England, 1784* (The *Mélanges sur l'Angleterre* of François de la Rochefoucauld), ed. by Jean Marchand and trans. by S. C. Roberts, 1933, p. 30.

[2] Sheraton, in the *Cabinet Dictionary*, remarks: 'That, however, which is generally distinguished by Spanish mahogany is finer than what is called Cuba. . . .'

[3] *The Dictionary of English Furniture*, revised ed. by Ralph Edwards, 1954, vol. II, p. 296.

[4] *Gillow Letterbooks*, 15 May 1775.

which runs up to it'), was, according to Sheraton, 'the principal kind of mahogany in use amongst cabinet-makers' — despite its inferior quality, its softness and tendency to mark and fade.[1] It was obtainable in larger boards and planks, was lighter (both in colour and weight) and more easily worked. 'The grain of Honduras wood', he observes, 'is of a different quality from that of Cuba, which is close and hard, without black speckles, and of a rosy hue, and sometimes strongly figured; but Honduras wood is of an open nature, with black or grey spots, and frequently of a more flashy figure than Spanish. The best quality of Honduras wood is known by its being free from chalky and black speckles, and when the colour is inclined to a dark gold hue. The common sort of it looks brisk at a distance, and of a lively pale red; but, on close inspection, is of an open and close grain, and of a spongy appearance.'

SATINWOOD

Satinwood was imported from both West and East Indies, and was employed in the solid (for chairs, for example, about 1800) and largely as a veneer. It ranges in colour from a pale yellow to deep orange, is close grained and takes a brilliant polish; and it is found plain and richly figured. The East Indian variety was known also as 'Manilla wood', from the name of the capital of the Philippine Islands.

Satinwood was considered 'highly valuable' amongst cabinet-makers. Sheraton, in 1803, refers to its having been 'much in requisition among people of fashion for above 20 years past' on account of its 'cool, light, and pleasing effect in furniture'. It provided a suitable ground for inlaid decoration (it is often banded by a contrasting dark wood, or inlaid with panels of other woods) or for painted ornament; and its period of popularity coincides with successive fashions for marquetry and painted furniture. Sheraton distinguishes the wood obtained from the West Indies (which had, in fact, been introduced into favour as early as about 1765) as being softer, sometimes paler in colour (at that date, a most desirable quality), more boldly figured and, because of its greater breadth, more serviceable. 'The East India wood', he states, 'runs narrow, and is used in general only for cross banding'; but of it he writes: 'I think no instance in nature, yet discovered, does exceed the beauty of the richest sort of it.' Many of his designs, in particular those

---

[1] A faded wood was not admired by Sheraton's contemporaries. Fading is a characteristic of poor quality wood.

for drawing-room furniture and ladies' pieces, were intended for execution in satin-wood. After 1800, satinwood was supplanted in fashion by rosewood, and other dark woods, which, strikingly marked, contrasted effectively with brass inlay and mounts.

HAREWOOD

Harewood, known as 'silverwood' in the later eighteenth century, was employed as a ground veneer, often in conjunction with satinwood, for commodes and other pieces with elaborate inlaid decoration. It is actually a veneer of sycamore or maple (which are of the same genus) stained with oxide of iron and is of a greenish-grey colour, which becomes golden with age. It has a distinctive figure (corresponding to that of the cut of sycamore used in the manufacture of violins), which is termed 'fiddle back'.

BEECH

Beech was in extensive demand in London and in the country, being employed usually for painted furniture, as well as for carcase work, as the seat rails of chairs, settees and bed frames. Sheraton writes: 'It is brought to London in great quantities from 1 inch boards to 5 inch planks, and is now the cheapest wood in use.'

DEAL

Deal is not a species of wood but a term (from Low German: *dele*, plank, floor) applied to boards of pine or fir, first imported from Frisia and the Baltic. 'Deal', observes a writer in 1804, 'is the wood of the fir tree, and is chiefly brought from Sweden, Norway, and other northern European countries. . . . The Norway fir produces the white deal commonly used by carpenters: from this pitch is also drawn; whence it takes its second name.'[1] Yellow deal, being soft and free from knots and forming an excellent ground for veneers, was extensively used for carcase work in the seventeenth and eighteenth centuries. It was to an extent super-seded by red deal after about 1750.

[1] *The Book of Trades or Library of the Useful Arts*, printed for Tabart and Co., London, 1804, Pt. I, p. 49.

PINE

Pinus Strobus, a white wood known not as deal but pine, was imported from North America at the end of the century and largely used in the construction of cheap mahogany furniture. *Pinus resinosa*, a red pine, was also the product of North America.

THE PRICES OF WOODS

Satinwood, substantially more expensive (by about 2s. 6d. in the pound) than the common Honduras mahogany, approximated in cost to the best Cuban wood, and to sacquebu or sabicu (a hard, tough wood, of chestnut-brown colour with darker stripes, resembling mahogany), also obtained from Cuba.

Among the woods employed as contrasting veneers and for inlays were: amboyna and thuya (imported respectively from the West Indies and North Africa, but of much the same appearance), kingwood, tulip wood (often used with satinwood, and, when new, pinkish in colour), rosewood, purple-wood, snake wood, zebra-wood, yew and maple. These were again more costly, and were generally required only in small quantities, as for bandings. To the list may be added walnut, holly, pear and other fruit woods, laburnum and ebony. A green wood, now faded in colour, was beech or pear, treated with an oxide of copper.

Some grades of Honduras mahogany and cedar were both used occasionally, for furniture of high quality, for drawer linings, wardrobe shelves and the insides of secretary drawers, as a substitute for wainscot oak, or for deal. Sheraton remarks 'a common kind of cedar, in colour much like dark mahogany', which, he says, 'does very well for the bottoms and backs of common drawer work, particularly for bottoms, as it comes cheap, and often broad enough to do without jointing.' His observation that 'it comes cheap' is obscure, since it would seem that an extra charge obtained for pieces so made.

There was wide variation in the quality of furniture supplied by different makers, and in different localities — as well as in that produced in one and the same shop. Quality was related to cost, and cost depended on the value of the materials employed and on labour charges. Wages were still low, and the lesser factor, but furniture of good workmanship, if elaborately shaped and ornamented, required many days in its making. The main decorative processes were carving and turning; veneering, marquetry and inlay; gilding, painting and japanning.

CARVING

Carving, as a means of decoration, had fallen into comparative disuse about 1765, with the revival of marquetry. The carved ornament, for example, found on the backs of late eighteenth-century mahogany parlour chairs is sparingly employed, and on a small scale (Plate 10). The mouldings of case furniture are often plain, without a carved running pattern (Plate 77). By the last decade of the century, however, marquetry was in turn superseded in large part by painting or japanning, which provided colour decoration at less labour and expense.

PAINTING AND JAPANNING

Decorated furniture of this kind falls roughly into two classes: furniture, usually of satinwood, with painted ornaments (Colour Plates B and D and Plates 32, 73), and furniture made from an inferior wood, such as birch or beech, painted over with a ground colour — popularly black, cream or green (Plates 20, 88). The latter may be termed, with convenience, 'japanned'.

Hepplewhite, in 1788, speaks of 'the new and very elegant fashion . . . arisen within these few years' of finishing chairs 'with painted or japanned work, which gives a rich and splendid appearance to the minuter parts of the ornaments, which are generally thrown in by the painter'. He adds that 'japanned chairs should have cane bottoms, with linen or cotton cases over cushions to accord with the general hue of the chair'. Japanned seat furniture was generally caned. The re-employment of caning coincided with the revived interest in this form of decoration.[1]

By the close of the century, japanned furniture enjoyed a considerable vogue and there existed in London a number of 'Japan Chair' manufactories, selling not

[1] The term 'japanning' had been applied at the beginning of the century to European lacquer work, in imitation of the Oriental. The technique which now obtained was inferior and equivalent to varnish painting.

only drawing room, parlour and bedroom chairs, but sofas, bed and window cornices, and card, Pembroke and toilet tables.

Sheraton, like Hepplewhite, does not distinguish between japanned and painted furniture. Referring in the *Cabinet Dictionary* to 'japanning' as 'a kind of painting', he remarks the colours used to be 'precisely the same as those for good oil painting' and instances 'white', 'lakes', 'Prussian blue', 'vermilion' and 'verdigrise'.

MARQUETRY, INLAYING AND VENEERING

Sheraton's observations (which bear on the popularity of japanned furniture) that 'inlaying, in cabinet-making', had been 'much in use between twenty and thirty years back' but 'laid aside, as a very expensive mode of ornamenting furniture, as well as being subject to a speedy decay', must be taken to refer to marquetry, which is an elaborate process and may be described as the assembling and inlaying of cut veneers of various decorative woods in a darker veneered ground (Plate 72).

Veneering, done by hammer or caul, and inlaying remained essential techniques, employed for most articles of furniture of mahogany or satinwood of good quality. Sheraton defines veneering as 'the art of laying down and gluing very thin cut wood, of a fine quality and valuable, upon common wood'. He states that its object is 'cheapness, and sometimes appearance', but adds that 'the ground, glue, and extra time are equivalent to the expence of solid wood, except it be to save very rich solid boards'. Cabinet-makers relied for decorative effect on the use of contrasting veneers and bandings. The doors of cabinets, bookcases and wardrobes, which centred sometimes in oval or diamond-shaped panels (Plates 68, 69, 85), were thus relieved. Fine strings of box, sycamore or other light coloured wood, and of black wood, were commonly employed as ornament throughout the last quarter of the eighteenth century (Plate 33A); towards about 1800, the inlay was more frequently of black wood, or of brass, and was sometimes arranged in geometrical patterns (Plates 40B, 64). Inlaying with brass was said to be most durable and to look well let into dark woods of any kind. Sheraton himself had recommended the use of brass at an early date (see note on Plate 39).

STRINGING AND PANELLING

Stringing was very generally applied to the straight taper leg of square section (the 'Marlbro'' leg), whether plain or with moulded ('thermed') foot, to the stump foot and to the 'top edge' and sides of 'claws' (Plates 61, 86). Such supports, if not decorated with reeds or flutes, were sometimes 'panelled'. 'Panelling' properly consisted of sinking and letting in a panel, with or without a bordering string (Plate 7). 'Panelling', however, was effectively simulated by means of strings inlaid in a flush surface and, as such, was a most popular device (Plates 60, 63). An ornament of 'panels formed with strings' is, for example, frequently to be found on the frames of card, Pembroke and pier tables. The 'panels' were variously shaped, being 'square', made with rounded or with astragal ends, with canted or with hollow corners.

BANDING

A variety of exotic woods were used for bandings, which had become broader and ranged normally from a quarter of an inch to three inches in width (Plate 34). In straight-banding, the wood was cut along the length of the grain; in cross-banding, across the grain.[1] The latter was the more usually employed, but more expensive, because the bands were necessarily made up of short lengths of veneer, which required jointing. Bands were often bordered by stringing lines on one or both sides. Banding 'in solid work' was rather more laboriously effected than in a veneer ground. Banding on 'straight work' was a comparatively simple matter; the process was more difficult when the bands were themselves curved, as for the surrounds of oval, circular or serpentine table tops, or were to be let into shaped surfaces, when, that is, the banding was 'on hollow or round work'.

FLUTING

Fluting, still very generally employed as an ornament in the years preceding the Regency, was of two distinct kinds: inlaid (Plate 40A) and 'common' fluting

[1] Feather-banding, wherein the wood was cut at an angle between the two, was still used, occasionally, at this period (Plate 68).

(Plate 31). Inlaid flutes (usually satinwood in mahogany, or vice versa) were used to decorate the friezes of tables and sideboards, the flat surfaces of 'Marlbro'' legs or features such as pilasters; they were less suitable for turned legs or, for example, the pillars of pedestal tables. Inlaid flutes were sometimes shaded. 'Common flutes', grooves cut in the solid wood, were the more readily worked and were produced, roughly, at half the cost of inlaid flutes of comparable size.

REEDING

Reeding, a moulding which is the reverse of fluting, was increasingly preferred towards the end of the century. Reeding, in point of strength, was somewhat superior to fluting, which it tended to replace on chair and table legs (particularly if these were of cylindrical form), on chair arms, bedposts, etc. (Plates 6, 28A, 37D). It was considered appropriate that the number of reeds worked on a flat surface should be odd and, otherwise, that one reed should occupy a central position 'facing the eye'. Spiral reeding was used also with good effect (Plate 24).

MOULDING

The structural parts of case furniture, such as the cornice, frieze or plinth, or the framings, were emphasized and effectively displayed by mouldings, worked either in the solid or on applied strips. The required profiles were obtained either by moulding planes or by scratch stocks. The cost of the work was appreciably greater if the profile was complex, and was doubled, or more, if the moulding required was for a curved or serpentine surface. Mouldings were worked both 'long-way' (with the grain) and 'cross-way' — the latter a more difficult task. To take an instance: the price per foot for working a moulded cornice on 'straight work', with the grain, was quadrupled for 'serpentine work' across the grain.

D. Satinwood commode, with painted decoration; c. 1790.

Victoria and Albert Museum.

THE FURNITURE OF 'THE DRAWING BOOK'

CHAIRS

The numerous designs for 'Parlour' and 'Drawing Room' chairs and for chair backs, illustrated in the *Drawing Book*, compare favourably with those produced by Hepplewhite for the *Guide*; the type of chair shown, moreover, is comparatively new. Sheraton's inventive powers at this time were considerable, and his adverse, sharp criticism of the *Guide* had some measure of justification: '. . . notwithstanding the late date of Heppelwhite's book', he writes, 'if we compare some of the designs, particularly the chairs, with the newest taste, we shall find that this work has already caught the decline, and perhaps, in a little time, will suddenly die in the disorder.'

In the 1790's, chairs in 'the newest taste' were of rectilinear form (Plates 6, 8). Sheraton favours square backs in preference to those of oval, heart or shield shape, which hitherto had been in fashion and which continued to be made throughout the decade (Colour Plate B). The change of style is marked; it is, nevertheless, exampled by certain surviving chairs dating from the 1780's (Plate 7), and, significantly, by several designs in the *Guide*, dated 1787, two of which at least, are of 'Sheraton' type (Plate 10). Sheraton's designs are agreeably varied within the somewhat narrow limits he chose to adopt. They give the impression of having been conceived by one man, and it does not seem likely that he was indebted here to others. The chairs are elegant and well proportioned, and the distribution of ornament judicious.

In general, the filling of the chair back is left fairly open and consists of an arrangement of upright bars, or balusters, so disposed as to divide the area into three main, vertical parts; often, these bars are grouped at the centre to form, in effect, an open splat contained within straight uprights. The filling has always a pronounced vertical emphasis, in so far as the design permits. The member which corresponds to the shoe piece, which is to be found in many examples, is attached to a straight bottom rail and not to the chair seat, as at an earlier period. The bottom rail is narrow and, as was common practice, usually raised a few inches above the seat. The cresting rail, at least for 'Parlour' chairs, is again narrow and usually either straight or raised in the centre; in few instances is the rail bowed or shaped.[1] The arm rests are set high and join the back uprights at an acute angle close to the cresting rail; their supports form an extension of the front legs and are perpendicular. (They are not shaped as a concave curve to sweep backwards and upwards from the cappings on the legs, as had been customary, nor are they secured to the side rails of the seats — a construction still used at this period.)

Sheraton distinguishes clearly between 'Parlour' and 'Drawing Room' chairs. 'The general style of furnishing a dining-parlour', he states, 'should be in substantial and useful things, avoiding trifling ornaments and unnecessary decorations' and the furniture, without exception, 'of mahogany, as being the most suitable for such apartments.' For chairs, he recommends, with reservations, the use of 'Spanish or Cuba' mahogany 'of a clean, straight grain', observing that 'wood of this quality will rub bright, and keep cleaner than any Honduras wood'. The 'Drawing Room' chairs, on the other hand, are intended to be painted and gilt, or japanned. Of two examples illustrated in Plate XXXII (Plate 12) he writes: 'These chairs are finished in white and gold, or the ornaments may be japanned; but the French finish them in mahogany, with gilt mouldings. . . . Chairs of this kind have an effect which far exceeds any conception we can have of them from an uncoloured engraving, or even of a coloured one.' Two designs for 'Drawing Room' chairs, comparable with these last, are included in the *Appendix*, Plate VI, again with directions for finishing. The first of these chairs, it is suggested, 'may be finished in Japan painting, interspersed with a little gilding . . . which has a lively effect'. The second, 'with seat and back covered with printed silk' is of somewhat different character; and the frame is proposed to be finished in burnished gold. 'The legs and stumps', observes Sheraton, 'have twisted flutes and fillets, done in the turning, which produce a good effect in the gold.'

'Drawing Room' chairs, unlike 'Parlour' chairs, which are straight-fronted, are shown with shaped or rounded seats. The legs are turned, and reeded or fluted, with a well-defined taper towards the foot; and often the arm supports, back uprights and other members are also turned. 'Parlour' chairs, however, retain frequently the square taper legs, sometimes moulded or 'panelled', that were

---

[1] Sheraton, in Plate LX, illustrates 'A Dining Parlour in imitation of the Prince of Wales's' at Carlton House, of which he had had a 'very transient view' (Plate 96A). He describes the chairs as 'of mahogany, made in the style of the French, with broad top-rails hanging over each back foot; the legs are turned, and the seats covered with red leather'.

fashionable in the 1780's; and, similarly, the uprights are usually flat and moulded Their design is reticent and comparatively severe.

Sheraton includes also various designs for 'Backs for Painted Chairs'. The fashion for painted furniture was widespread, and many painted or japanned chairs of late eighteenth-century date survive. They are made usually of beech wood, with caned seats (plane, however, a tough, white wood, with a close grain, was used as an alternative to beech in many country districts). The painted ornament, confined to narrow surfaces such as the uprights, top rail or splat, and delicately executed, is predominantly floral (Plate 15); although subsequently, from about 1795, small figure subjects were introduced on oblong or oval tablets when these became a feature of the design (Plate 9). Chairs of this description were intended for general use in smaller drawing rooms, the 'tea-room' and elsewhere.[1] They do not resemble the formal 'Drawing Room' chairs, particularized by Sheraton, which are also proposed for painting. By contra-distinction Sheraton's designs for 'Parlour' and painted chairs are, to some extent, interchangeable. The latter are more elaborate and provide for painted detail, but, with modification, are suitable for rendering in mahogany or in satinwood, again with painted ornament. Of one such design, Sheraton remarks, it 'may be either a drawing-room chair painted, or it may be made a handsome parlour chair by taking out the top drapery and making the bottom of the banister plain'.

These various designs in the *Drawing Book*, most of which were executed in or before 1793, are by no means comprehensive: they reflect Sheraton's individual preferences. Rightly described by their author as being 'in the newest taste' they nevertheless do not provide an adequate summary of contemporary production.

The form of chair, with square back, which was then commonly adopted, admits of very varied treatment. Sheraton, as has been said, favours as a filling an arrangement of vertical bars, which he groups with good effect. Equally popular is an upright diagonal lattice, filling the area (Plate 13), or, as the century draws to a close and the chair back tends to become lower, a filling which consists of a low, horizontal lattice, contained within horizontal bars (which are comparatively closely spaced), supporting an entablature. Sometimes, an oblong or oval panel is incorporated in the back (Plate 9), or, alternatively, a diagonal crossing, centring

[1] Sheraton, in his directions for furnishing the 'Tea-room', given in the *Cabinet Dictionary*, refers somewhat disparagingly to painted chairs: 'The tea-room or breakfast-room may abound with beaufets, painted chairs, flower-pot stands, hanging book shelves . . . and all the little things which are engaging to the juvenile mind.'

in a *patera*, is its most prominent feature. The emphasis to the design, in these latter cases, is horizontal. Some of these characteristics are to be seen in the japanned beech wood armchair in the Victoria and Albert Museum (Plate 15). The chair is lightly constructed and of meagre proportions, but has features of style that foreshadow the full Regency. Seen in side elevation, the back uprights and rear legs form a wide, continuous curve, bisected at the level of the seat, opposing that of the legs in front; there is an outward, backward roll to the top rail.

The change of taste which occurred in the course of the first quarter of the nineteenth century is thus described by Sir Walter Scott (*Quarterly Review*, March 1828): 'Our national taste indeed', he writes, 'has been changed, in almost every particular, from that which was meagre, formal, and poor, and has attained, comparatively speaking, a character of richness, variety, and solidity. An ordinary chair, in the most ordinary parlour, has now something of an antique cast — something of Grecian massiveness, at once, and elegance in its forms. That of twenty or thirty years since was mounted on four tapering and tottering legs, resembling four tobacco-pipes; the present supporters of our stools have a curule air, curve outwards behind, and give a comfortable idea of stability to the weighty aristocrat or ponderous burgess. . . .'

Sheraton recognizes the change in his later designs for chairs in the *Cabinet Dictionary*. They are, however, strained for invention and relatively undistinguished.

Sheraton makes no mention in the *Drawing Book* of hall chairs, although these articles (and benches and corridor stools) were widely produced. They were, as he remarks later in the *Cabinet Dictionary*, such as were 'placed in halls, for the use of servants or strangers waiting on business . . . generally made all of mahogany, with turned seats, and the crest or arms of the family painted on the centre of the back'. Their design is distinct from that of other varieties of chair. The specimen reproduced (Plate 11) is typical. They were not made for comfort and were un-upholstered.

STOOLS

Stools also are neglected in the *Drawing Book* — and, under this heading, in the *Cabinet Dictionary*. No significant development in their design occurred before about 1800, when the attempt was made to reproduce more exactly the forms of classical antiquity with the re-introduction of the 'X' pattern (cp. Plates 22, 23). He prefers instead to offer two designs for a 'conversation chair' — a novel form of seat made with a wide, deep seat, narrowing at its junction with the back. The occupant sat with his legs across the seat, facing the back, and resting his arms on a padded top rail. The 'conversation chair', says Sheraton, 'is peculiarly adapted for this kind of idle position, as I venture to call it, which is by no means calculated to excite the best of conversation.' Such chairs (known as *voyeuses*) were used in France by spectators at card playing.

SETTEES, ETC.

The stylistic development of settees, whether of chair-back form or upholstered or caned, corresponds with that of chairs. The lines of the settee became increasingly severe during the last decade of the century, and the back **was** often straight, although in some cases centring in a long oblong panel, or cresting (Plate 20). 'If the top rail', observes Sheraton of one of two upholstered settees illustrated in the *Drawing Book* and *Appendix*, 'be thought to have too much work, it can be finished in a straight rail, as the design shews.' These pieces, which he designates as 'sofas' (the terms were more or less interchangeable, and still are), are comparable with contemporary French models (Plate 21). Their sides, as well as the cushioned backs and seats, are filled in with upholstery and are fronted by turned supports which form a continuation of the outside legs. The arms, as with drawing-room chairs, are provided with padded rests, or *manchettes*.

Sheraton shows also two designs for *chaises longues*. 'These articles', he states, 'have their name from the French, which imports a long chair. Their use is to rest or loll upon after dinner. . . .' The more typical of the two is framed in two parts. 'The end, or chair part, is made to receive the stool part within its sides; and the sides of the stool part screw in against the inside of the chair.' Pieces also fashionable at the time were the *confidante* and the *duchesse*. Both were of a composite nature: the *confidante* was formed as a settee, with attached 'Barjier' chairs at the ends; while the component parts of the *duchesse* were two facing chairs with a stool in the middle (Plate 19).[1] *Duchesses*, although for some years a fashionable article of furniture, have rarely survived, and it would seem likely that, when

[1] The term '*duchesse*' referred also to a kind of bed.

practicable, the several parts of the *duchesse* were often put to separate use, and have been dispersed.

PIER TABLES, COMMODES OR 'ENCLOSED PIER TABLES' AND CARD TABLES

Pier tables, which were designed to stand beneath a glass between tall windows, were primarily decorative pieces. They were much in demand for drawing rooms and 'not being applied to such general use as other Tables' admitted, 'with great propriety' (writes Hepplewhite in the *Guide*) 'of much elegance and ornament'. Pier and side tables were often made of satinwood, with inlaid or painted decoration, or of a soft wood, japanned and painted (Colour Plate C); the frames were sometimes gilt (Plates 28, 29). Mahogany examples were comparatively plain, with carved or inlaid ornament.

Sheraton states that the tops were 'most commonly veneered in rich satin, or other valuable wood, with a cross-band on the outside, a border about two inches richly japanned, and a narrow cross-band beyond it, to go all round'; alternatively, the tops were of marble and the frames of 'gold, or white and burnished gold'.

Pier tables were variously shaped, being popularly semi-circular; bow-fronted, with straight ends; break-fronted; and straight-fronted, with ovolo corners. Such shapes permitted of considerable modification. Sheraton illustrates two elegant tables (one of a shallow, broken 'D'-shape; the other with serpentine middle, rounded corners and short, straight ends). Each is supported on two centre and two end legs of cylindrical form, tied by curved stretchers. Characteristically, the end legs are brought forward and serve to accent and frame the shaped front. 'Stretcher rails', he observes, 'have of late been introduced to these tables, and it must be owned that it is with good effect, as they take off the long appearance of the legs, and make the under part appear more furnished; besides they afford an opportunity of fixing a vase or basket of flowers, which, with their reflection when there is a glass behind, produces a brilliant appearance.'

The glass, to which he refers, was 'fixed either in the dado of the room; or in the frame of the table' and appeared to be an extension of the mirror surmounting the table.

The pier table which Sheraton reproduces in one of his two views of the

'Chinese Drawing Room' in Carlton House (Plate XXXI of the *Appendix* to the *Drawing Book*) is not in the prevailing taste. In form, it resembles a French *étagère* with open shelves. It is probably of French origin, and may be the work of Adam Weisweiler (working *c.* 1778–*c.* 1809), who successfully survived the Revolution. He was largely employed by the *marchand-mercier*, Daguerre, and this influential dealer supplied French furniture for the Prince's use at Carlton House. Its inclusion in the *Drawing Book* is of interest as affording evidence of a source of influence on Sheraton (Plate 27).

Drawing-room commodes (to be distinguished from 'dressing commodes' or 'commode chests-of-drawers') were likewise intended 'chiefly for ornament, to stand under a glass' and designed on much the same plan as pier tables. They were sometimes described as 'enclosed pier tables'. Before 1790, the majority were semi-circular (or semi-circular with hollow or with ogee ends). Often, they were made of satinwood, with inlaid or painted ornament, and provided with a cupboard, or cupboards, fitted with shelves enclosed by a principal door in front or one at each end, and supported on taper stump feet; see Plate 30 and Colour Plate D.

Card tables were generally made with hinged double tops. When not in use, they were placed against a wall, resembling small side or pier tables.[1] Usually, the folding half top was supported, when the table was opened, either on a single gate-leg, pivoting on the back framing, or on two such legs (known as 'fly feet'). The standard forms were square; circular (or oval); serpentine; and straight-fronted with curved (concave) corners. From about 1795, a straight-fronted table with rounded (convex) corners was popular; the shape of the half top approximating to a narrow 'D'.

Sheraton shows two elegantly elaborated designs for card tables: one, with panelled square taper legs, is of this latter type; the other, a bow-fronted table with square corners has projecting, cylindrical supports, positioned at the angles.

The straight taper legs found on these tables were of either square or round section. The latter form was the more fashionable in the last decade of the century, and generally the more expensive. Sheraton, in the *Accompaniment* (Plate IX), gives six patterns for 'Legs for Pier and Card Tables'. They are of an intricate nature and unlikely to have been executed without modification, but it may be

---

[1] William Moore, setting up as cabinet-maker in Dublin after 'long experience at Messrs. Mayhew and Ince, London', advertises, among other articles for sale, 'Card Tables on a new construction (both ornamented and plain) which appear like small Pier Tables' (*Dublin Evening Post*, 1782).

significant that those suggested for pier tables (the more decorative piece) are cylindrical, richly carved and intended for gilding; whereas those for card tables, which are to be ornamented with inlaid panels and stringing, are of square section. However, in practice, legs of identical pattern and of either form were adapted indiscriminately to pier and card tables, and to some other articles of furniture; and the proportions were altered to suit particular requirements (Plate 48).

PEMBROKE AND SOFA TABLES

Pembroke tables were exceedingly useful small pieces, serving variously for meals, for writing and as work tables (Plate 34). Their name, according to Sheraton, was derived from that 'of the lady who first gave orders for one of them, and who probably gave the first idea of such a table to the workmen' — presumably the Countess of Pembroke, soon after the middle of the century.

The Pembroke table was made with an extending top, being provided with two flaps, which were rule-jointed, supported on hinged wooden brackets. It was generally of oval or rectangular form, although, from about 1790, a rectangular table with rounded corners (that is, with 'D' shaped ends) was popular. The 'bed' commonly measured about 2 ft. 3 in. and the top, when extended, 3 ft., and more, in length. Sheraton observes that the height should never exceed 2 ft. 4 in., 'including castors' — a condition not always observed in practice. There was one deep drawer in the frame. The Pembroke table had usually four taper legs of square section, but an alternative form of support, employed in the 1790's, consisted of 'a pillar and claws'. Sheraton shows a design for a table of this kind (Plate LIV of the *Drawing Book*), of which he remarks: 'the manufacturing part . . . differs but very little from those in common use.' The workman is 'desired to observe that the top of the table, as shewn in the design, is not meant to represent a regular ellipsis, as they are generally made a little fuller out at each corner of the bed. The reason of this is, that the flaps, when turned down, may better hide the joint rail'. He devotes considerably more attention to the 'Harlequin Pembroke Table' (Plate LVI), a composite piece designed 'not only as a breakfast, but also as a writing table, very suitable for a lady'. The table, which is rectangular, is constructed with a 'till', or rising desk of small drawers and pigeon holes, seated below the fixed top and occupying half the area contained by a specially deep framing, the other half being given up to two drawers, one above the other. The 'till' is 'raised and lowered by turning the fly-bracket which supports the flap, yet the bracket is made to lose this effect or power by the turn of a key, and the bracket may then be drawn out to support the flap without raising the till, and the table can then be used, as in common, to breakfast upon'. Sheraton gives the credit for this particular design to a friend, from whom he received his 'first ideas of it'. Harlequin tables of different kinds had, in fact, been made for some years: a design, dated 1788, for an ingenious combination dressing and writing table, with hinged box lid, which is of this description, had appeared in the first edition of the *Book of Prices*.

Sofa tables, which were made in large numbers in the early nineteenth century, were extended on the same principle as Pembroke tables, from which they were evolved and which they superseded (see note on Plate 43). They were normally of rectangular form, with rounded corners, being 5 ft., or more, in length when opened and about 2 ft. broad, and were fitted with two drawers in the frame. They were constructed with ornamental end supports, sometimes lyre-shaped, or standards, united by a turned horizontal rail, or, alternatively, rested on a central support rising from a platform with curved 'claws'. They were intended to be placed before a sofa, as their description implies, and were occupied by ladies chiefly 'to draw, write, or read upon'. They were doubtless used also for meals. The tops of some later tables were fitted with a sliding panel disclosing a back-gammon or chess board.

DINING TABLES

The *Drawing Book* shows no design for a dining table. Sheraton, like Hepplewhite and, at an earlier date, Chippendale, disregards this article of furniture as one providing little scope for invention — apart from some incidental observations.

The common dining table, with rectangular top, made 'with one or two flaps to ditto hung with rule or square joints, four plain Marlbro' legs, [and] one fly on each side', cost little more than a shilling per foot. ('The length and width' were, for costing, 'added together'.)[1] Its construction resembled that of the gate-leg table. Often, two or more such tables, or sections, were supplied to fit together

[1] The *Book of Prices*, 1793: the basic price is 1s. 2d. per foot.

to form one long table, which might be extended at will, according to their number and the use made of the flaps, and were joined by means of 'tongues and mortices', 'spring and staple fastenings' or 'hinge and button fastenings'. The dining table, when set out in its several sections, was generally spoken of as a 'set' or 'range' of dining tables.

The tops of single tables were variously shaped. Frequently, the flaps were rounded at the corners, or were 'swept either serpentine or circular' (semi-circular). Oval tables, which had been fashionable about 1780, continued to be made, and those with semi octagonal ends, which it would seem, had lost favour about that time. (Gillow's, in a letter dated 1778, refer to an oval form as being 'now the most esteemed, where only one table is wanted', and, at a later date, to 'octagon ends' as being 'quite out of fashion, and neither half so handsome or convenient as half circles or half ovals'.)

A popular form of sectional dining table was made in three parts and consisted of a rectangular centre, with extension flaps, and a pair of semi-circular ends, each having also, usually, a single flap. The ends (when not in use) were stood against a wall and served independently as side tables. Alternatively, the ends combined, without the centre, to form a dining table of variable size. Such tables were supplied by leading makers throughout the second half of the century. France and Beckwith, 'Upholsterers and Cabinet makers to His Majesty' (*q.v.*), as late as 1791, received £24 for 'a set of Mahogany dining tables, consisting of one square frame with 2 flaps and 2 round ends with a flap to each all made to take off with strap hinges, bolt and fork fastenings, the whole or any part to Join together at pleasure, good Jamaica wood'.[1] Jane Austen, in a letter of 1800, refers to the family's having newly acquired a set of tables, and to their arrangement — which was unorthodox: 'The tables are come, and give general contentment. I had not expected that . . . we should so well agree in the disposition of them; but nothing except their own surface can have been smoother. The two ends put together form one constant table for everything, and the centre piece stands exceedingly well under the glass, and holds a great deal most commodiously without looking awkwardly.'[2]

The majority of dining tables made towards the close of the century were, however, of the type known as 'Pillar-and-Claw' tables, and stood, not on taper legs, but on central supports, terminating in short legs, or 'claws' (Plate 37).

[1] Royal Household Accounts, 1791.
[2] J. E. Austen-Leigh, *Memoir of Jane Austen*, with introd. and notes by R. W. Chapman, 1951, p. 61.

Sheraton, in his description of 'A Dining Parlour in imitation of the Prince of Wales's' at Carlton House (Plate LX), refers to the 'large range of dining-tables, standing on pillars with four claws each, which', he says, 'is now the fashionable way of making these tables' (Plate 96A). Some ten years later, in the *Cabinet Dictionary*, naming tables of this kind as 'common' and 'useful', he observes that they may be made 'to any size, by having a sufficient quantity of pillar and claw parts, for between each of these is a loose flap, fixed by means of iron straps and buttons, so that they are easily taken off and put aside; and the beds may be joined to each other with brass fork or strap fastenings'. He suggests that the size may readily be calculated 'by allowing 2 feet to each person sitting at table'. He considers that a single dining table for eight persons should measure '5 feet by 4', or a little less, 'at which two upon each side may sit'.

Such methods of enlargement, accepted for many years, were not wholly satisfactory (as providing insufficient leg room for sitters) and about this time a number of devices for extending tables were invented and patented. Sheraton, in 1803, refers to some of the various sorts of dining tables in use as being 'under the protection of his Majesty's patent'. He distinguishes between two tables under patent, the frames of which 'are made to draw out, and loose flaps are inserted between those [flaps] which are fixed on the drawing part' and one, a pillar and claw table wherein 'the drawing part by which it is increased in length is in the block to which the pillar is fixed. . . .' Of the former he writes: 'the superiority of the one to the other chiefly consists in the portableness of its parts, having the flaps to inclose in the part which draws out, and the legs to screw off and inclosed with them.' The pillar and claw table also suffers from this disadvantage: 'the loose flaps . . . must be, when not used, put into some convenient place in the room where the dining table stands.'

Richard Gillow's patent, taken out in 1800, consisted 'in attaching to a table mounted upon a frame and legs or a pillar and claws wooden or metal sliders which run in dovetail T or square, or cylindrical, or other grooves, with or without wheels or rollers. The sliders are drawn out to the length required, and flaps are laid on them'. Other methods of enlargement were patented by Richard Brown (1805) and George Remington (1807). These tables were expanded on the 'lazy tongs' principle. Remington provides two legs to each division of the tongs, 'fixed in joints made of brass, iron, or any other suitable materials'.[1]

Tables of horseshoe shape were occasionally made. Shearer contributes a design

[1] *Abridgements of Specifications relating to Furniture and Upholstery*, 1869, Vol. 39.

for a 'Horseshoe Dining Table', dated 1788, to the *Book of Prices*. The table, segmental in shape, has folding flaps and extends to form a half circle. The recommended width is, as was usual, 2 ft. 6 in.

Most surviving horseshoe tables, however, are wine or social tables (and fitted with movable coasters attached to a brass rail), which were set before the fire after dinner. Another variety of social table was of kidney shape, and constructed in two separate parts (Plate 45).

THE 'UNIVERSAL' OR SLIDING-FLAP PEMBROKE TABLE

Sheraton's design for a 'Universal Table' is undistinguished and very simple, but the detailed notes that he gives are interesting for the information they provide on methods employed by contemporary craftsmen even for plain work. They confirm Adam Black's statement that he was bred to the 'cabinet business'. The piece is intended to be of use as both breakfast and dining table. It is square framed, supported on substantial, straight taper legs, with socket castors, and is extended by means of two draw leaves, fitted with raking sliders (Plate 38). The principle is that of the draw-table, introduced about the middle of the sixteenth century.

The 'universal table' was sometimes made with a single pull-out leaf. One such table is described in the Gillow records for 1790 as being 5 ft. 2 in. long, extended (the leaf measuring 14 in.).[1]

'CLAW' TABLES

The tripod form of support was very generally employed for small tea and occasional tables, as well as for such articles as pole screens, candle stands and music stands (Plate 56). Tripod tables, known at the time as 'claw' tables (when their construction follows that of the 'pillar and claw' parts of the dining table), were made with a variety of light tripod bases (Plate 49). Frequently an extra (fourth) claw was incorporated in the design.

Breakfast tables of this type would appear to have been introduced shortly before 1800 and soon to have become popular (Plate 37). 'Our breakfast table', explains Southey, in his *Letters from England*, 'is oval, large enough for eight or

[1] Estimate and Sketch Books, No. 572.

nine persons, yet supported upon one claw ['pillar and claw' part] in the centre. This is the newest fashion, and fashions change so often in these things, as well as in every thing else, that it is easy to know how long it is since a house has been fitted up, by the shape of the furniture.'[1]

SIDEBOARDS

'In spacious dining-rooms', observes Sheraton, 'the sideboards are often made without drawers of any sort, having simply a rail a little ornamented, and pedestals with vases at each end, which produce a grand effect.[2] One pedestal is used as a plate-warmer, and is lined with tin; the other as a pot-cupboard, and sometimes it contains a celleret for wine. The vases are used for water for the use of the butler, and sometimes as knife-cases. They are sometimes made of copper japanned, but generally of mahogany.' This type of sideboard, known as a sideboard table, was still fashionable at the date of publication of the *Drawing Book*.

The cellaret sideboard, a more useful piece and in consequence more popular, at least for smaller rooms, was introduced about the beginning of the last quarter of the century. It was in effect a composite piece, designed to take the place of sideboard table, pedestals and urns. Gillow's, in 1779, refer to this 'new sort of sideboard table now with drawers etc. in a genteel style to hold bottles', which, it is implied, was then being generally made. The cellaret sideboard offered obvious advantages. It was compactly formed, with fitted lateral drawers and cupboards, which were useful and commodious, and of neat and pleasing appearance. Hepplewhite, in the *Guide*, gives two designs for 'sideboards with drawers', which, he states, 'are often made to fit into a recess'. He says that 'the general custom is to make them from 5 and a half to 7 feet long, 3 feet high, from 28 to 32 inches wide'. He adds that 'the conveniences it affords render a dining-room incomplete without a sideboard'.

The distinction existing between these two types, which is sufficiently marked in so far as pieces of fine quality or the more elaborate 'book pieces' are concerned, is less readily to be applied to plain sideboards of the average sort. Small sideboard tables (some of which contain a shallow drawer, or drawers, wherein table linen was kept) were made for use in many households without accessory

---

[1] *Letters from England: by Don Manuel Alvarez Espriella. Translated from the Spanish*, 1807. The letters were written by Southey between 1803–7 and refer to a visit of 1802–3.

[2] The height of the pedestals coincides usually with that of the table.

pedestals and urns, as being preferable to cellaret sideboards. 'There are', notes Sheraton, 'other sideboards for small dining-rooms [made] without either drawers or pedestals; but they have generally a wine-cooper to stand under them, hooped with brass, partitioned and lined with lead, for wine bottles. . . .'

Standard forms both of the sideboard table and the cellaret sideboard are listed in the *Book of Prices*, and specimens are costed separately in detail. They are variously shaped, being 'straight-front', 'round-front' (bow-fronted), 'serpentine-front', 'circular' (semi-circular), made 'with Ovalo Corners', made 'with Eliptic Middle, and Eliptic Hollow on each Side,' made 'with Eliptic Middle, and Ogee on each Side' or 'with Hollow Middle, and Astragal on each Side'. Basically, the tables and cellaret sideboards approximate one to another; they are to be made to a common pattern but differ in size and in the provision or omission (as the case may be) of drawer and cupboard accommodation.[1] The several designs included (they are for cellaret sideboards) were contributed by Shearer and are dated 1788. They are, with one exception, of a workmanlike and entirely practical nature, being given to assist craftsmen in the execution of everyday orders.[2] That for 'A Circular Celleret Sideboard', which is illustrated in Plate 5, Fig. 1 of the second edition, is characteristic of the group (Plate 41). Small sideboards of this description, and those which are bow-fronted, would seem to have been made in large numbers. There is a fine example, which corresponds closely with Shearer's design, in the Lady Lever Art Gallery, at Port Sunlight (Plate 40A). Equally indicative of popular taste towards the close of the century is Shearer's coupled design (Fig. 2 of the same plate) for 'A Celleret Sideboard, with Eliptic Middle', with, alternatively, an 'Ogee' or an 'Eliptic Hollow' on each side (Plate 41). The construction to be followed is very similar to the foregoing, but such shaped pieces, because of the extra work involved in their making, were more expensive.

Sheraton's designs, which resemble those of Shearer (and of Hepplewhite) but are of a more elaborated and inventive cast, are all for pieces with drawers. A

---

[1] Invariably, the measurements of the 'standard' table are given as 4 ft. 6 in. long and 2 ft. 6 in. wide, with a 5 in. framing; whereas the cellaret sideboard is 5 ft. long with a 15 in. framing.

[2] The exception being Shearer's design for a large bow-fronted sideboard, with attached end pedestal cupboards and surmounting vases — the earliest published design for a sideboard of this kind. This commodious, but cumbersome, piece was intended for painted decoration.

The idea was developed by Sheraton, who shows in the *Appendix* a 'Side Board with Vase Knife Cases', made with an elliptic front and square pedestals, and fitted with an ornate scrolled brass back. 'The pedestal parts', he writes, 'may be made separate and then screwed to the sideboard.' The design is not one of his best.

straight-fronted sideboard, with rounded ends, shown in Plate XXVI of the *Drawing Book* (Plate 42), is provided with a brass gallery at the back 'to set large dishes against, and to support a couple of candle or lamp branches in the middle' — which, it is observed, 'when lighted, give a very brilliant effect to the silver ware'.[1] The cellaret, as was usual, is contained in the right-hand drawer and 'made to draw out separate from the rest. It is partitioned and lined with lead, to hold nine or ten wine bottles'. The drawer on the left 'is generally plain, but sometimes divided into two; the back division being lined with baize to hold plates, having a cover hinged to enclose the whole'. Both drawers are panelled to represent two, as was the common practice. The sideboard is substantial (according to the attached scale, it measures 7 ft. 6 in. in length). The ornamental tablet, carved with a spray of leaves, which is centred on the straight-fronted shallow drawer, is a *motif* frequently introduced by Sheraton in his designs for furniture, and here serves to break the long horizontal of the front. The sideboard is faced by square taper legs, with reeded decoration, which extend upwards from the lower edge of the side drawers and form, as it were, superimposed pilaster strips, enframing the front of the piece. The treatment is distinctive: characteristically, the legs (which may be regarded as the main vertical components of the design) are stressed. The centre part of the sideboard is thereby made the more prominent and the design given balance and stability.

Sheraton submits also a design for a large hollow-fronted sideboard, with rounded and shaped ends. 'If', he says, 'a sideboard be required nine or ten feet long, as in some noblemen's houses, and if the breadth of it be in proportion to the length, it will not be easy for a butler to reach across it. I therefore think, in this case, a hollow front would obviate the difficulty, and at the same time have a very good effect, by taking off part of the appearance of the great length of such a sideboard. Besides . . . the hollow front will sometimes secure the butler from the jostles of the other servants.' The sideboard is intended to be supported at the front by six 'engaged' legs, for which alternative patterns are shown. They are either 'turned the whole length, or rounded as far as the framing and turned below it, with carved leaves and flutes' or turned only below the framing — when the 'necks' are flat, and carved with pendant husks. This kind of sideboard, although 'not usual', was occasionally made and examples dating from these years, and from the early nineteenth century, have survived.

[1] These rods, by an indication in the index of plates, were to be obtained from 'Mr. Penton and Co. New-street Square, near St. Andrew's, Holborn'. 'Penton, Brass-founder', was a subscriber to the *Drawing Book*.

LIBRARY TABLES

'This piece', writes Sheraton of the oval 'Library Table' (Plate XXX of the *Drawing Book*), 'is intended for a gentleman to write on, or to stand or sit to read at, having desk-drawers at each end, and is generally employed in studies or library-rooms. It has already been executed for the Duke of York, excepting the desk-drawers, which are here added as an improvement' (Plate 39). The accompanying explanation of the design and directions for its execution are unusually detailed. The plate is oversize and one of the most elaborate in the *Drawing Book*. Clearly, Sheraton judged the piece to be one of special interest to his subscribers.

Kneehole pedestal library tables of a more conventional type (deriving from massive pieces of architectural character, which had been designed for the libraries of large Palladian houses) were at this period comparatively plain and of small dimensions (perhaps 3 to 4 ft. in length). They were often double-fronted (i.e. free-standing) and made of mahogany, with little or no ornament. In their simplest form these tables were straight-fronted, with end pedestals which were fitted with drawers or contained cupboards, and were supported on a low plinth or on bracket feet. Serpentine tables, with veneered serpentine ends and canted corners were, of course, more expensive.

'Kidney tables', so called from their 'resemblance to that intestine part of animals', would seem by this time to have come into very general use. 'Hepplewhite' contributes a design for a 'Knee-Hole Kidney Library Writing Table', dated 1792, to the *Book of Prices* (Plate 45). The table, at a basic price of £5 2s., is described as follows: 'Four feet long, two feet wide, veneer'd front and ends, four drawers in each wing, and one ditto above the knee hole, cock beaded, an astragal round the bottom of the carcase, on eight taper stump feet.' Among the numerous listed modifications or refinements that might be made at extra charge are: lining or veneering the top; making the table 'in three carcases'; 'veneering partition edges askew or cross-way' with 'king, tulip, or any other hard wood'; making with decorative pilasters to the front; making with 'a plinth round the bottom, in place of stump feet'; providing cupboards in the wings; and 'making the flap to rise with four stems, as shewn in plate' — an expensive extra.

The design closely resembles one, also dated 1792, published by Sheraton in the *Drawing Book* (Plate 44). There is no reason to believe that Hepplewhite was indebted to Sheraton for the idea of the piece, or vice versa, despite their similarity.

The Sheraton table, which is of more stilted proportions, is supported on turned stump feet and is fitted with pairs of handles to each drawer; it is constructed with a rising reading desk 'which slides out', and there are other small differences. Sheraton's conception, while less robust, is, characteristically, the more elegant of the two.

A popular and very distinctive form of writing or library table evolved by about 1790 was that known as the 'Carlton House Table' (Plate 46). The origin of the term has not been established but it would seem to have been in fairly general use by the closing years of the century. Sheraton illustrates one such table in the *Appendix* to the *Drawing Book*, but describes it as a 'Lady's Drawing & Writing Table'. The 'Carlton House Table', with small modifications, remained fashionable for more than twenty years. Indeed, a 'Hepplewhite' design for a table of this type, dated 1792, which first appears in the second edition of the *Book of Prices*, is included in all later issues, up to that of 1866. And it is possible that the design, even at this late date, served as a model for work.

Circular tables of an individual character, known as 'drum-top' tables, were also made before 1800. They are constructed with a central support in the form of a turned column with curved legs (a pillar and three, or four, claws) or, later, a column resting on a flat base (Plates 47, 55). The top, fitted with drawers (and dummy drawers) contained in the deep frieze, is made usually to revolve. These tables have the convenience that each drawer may be brought before the user as required. In some, the frieze was divided into partitions for books.

LADIES' WRITING TABLES

Small writing tables (called sometimes 'cabinets') and other light pieces intended specially for ladies' use, were made in considerable variety and numbers towards the end of the century (Plates 60, 61). Like work tables (Plates 50–52), 'writing fire screens' and 'trio' and 'quartetto' tables (Plate 54), they might be moved from place to place in a room; they were delicately and often very ingeniously formed, and sometimes were designed to serve a dual function (Plate 83). Fanny Burney writing to her father in September 1801, observes, 'no room looks really comfortable, or even quite furnished, without two tables — one to keep the wall and take upon itself the dignity of a little tidyness, the other to stand here, there, and everywhere, and hold letters and *make the agreeable* . . . a sort of table for a little work and a few books, *en gala* — without which, a room looks always forlorn.'[1]

The *Drawing Book* contains a number of designs for this class of furniture. One of these, for a 'Writing Table', illustrated in Plate XLIV of the *Drawing Book* (Plate 57A), resembles a design, dated 1792, which was contributed by 'Hepplewhite' to the second edition of the *Book of Prices* (Plate 57B). Most of the designs of the *Book of Prices*, because of their usefulness, are representative of varieties of furniture then commonly being produced in the workshops (Plate 61). They are not elaborated, nor do they exhibit the invention that, more often than not, is to be found in the *Drawing Book*.

Sheraton's design in this instance is relatively simple: he is content to show a small piece of conventional everyday character. The table is supported on plain taper legs of square section, with one long drawer in the framing. The drawer is fitted with a slider for writing and contains compartments for ink, sand and pens. The low superstructure of drawers and pigeon holes is made separately and is detachable. It is secured by a beading, let into the back and sides of the table top, and provided with a handle for lifting, fixed to the upper shelf. This latter refinement is one not to be found in the 'standard' table—if we may accept as 'standard' the 'Hepplewhite' design contained in the *Book of Prices*. Sheraton dispenses, too, with the arrangement whereby a writing flap, 'nine inches wide hing'd to the front' is 'supported by two lopers to draw out at the top of the legs' and substitutes a neat, fitted writing drawer. The drawer front itself is flush with the framing and cross-banded at the edges: the small cock bead (a moulding first introduced about 1730 and used throughout the mahogany period), popularly applied round the edges of the drawer fronts and forming a projecting rim, is omitted.

For this piece Sheraton recommends a width of no more than 20 in. — a considerable reduction in size, and one by which its elegant proportions are effectively determined. The vertical emphasis to the design obtained by this means is characteristic of Sheraton. (The increased depth of the writing drawer and, also, the elongated oval shape of the decorative vase *motif*, which is introduced in the back of the upper shelf, forming, as it were, a cresting, are contributory factors.)

Comparison may be made also with 'A Lady's Work Table', illustrated in the *Book of Prices*, Plate 25, Fig. 2 (Plate 56). The design for this table again is contributed by 'Hepplewhite', and dated 1792. The piece, clearly, corresponds very

[1] Letter of 6 September 1801, quoted by Constance Hill, *Juniper Hall*, 1904, pp. 258–9.

closely with the Sheraton 'Writing Table', in so far as its proportions and form are concerned, and the top is 'made to take off'. 'Hepplewhite', too, makes use of the vase *motif*, both as a feature of the back and of the (optional) ornamental, shaped stretcher. The table, which is not of the specialized pouch variety, nor constructed with a well, fitted with the various receptacles required by the needlewoman, is of the general sort intended 'for a little work and a few books'. Such tables were usually executed in satinwood, with some painted decoration.

WORK TABLES

Work tables made in the late eighteenth and early nineteenth centuries were generally designed with more regard to elegance than to serviceability. Three of several distinct varieties in use are here reproduced (Plates 50–52). The satinwood pouch table (Plate 50), fitted with a sliding fire screen, is perhaps most representative of popular taste. That, also of satinwood, of the '*tricoteuse*' type (Plate 51) is clearly inspired by French models. It bears a generic resemblance to Sheraton's design for a 'French Work Table', Plate LIV of the *Drawing Book*, but, in the form of the end standards, corresponds fairly closely with one of his two designs, dated 1793, for 'Pouch Tables', in the *Appendix*, Plate XXVI. The 'French Work Table', has a plain oblong tray top (the rim is hinged at one side and fastens by means of thumb springs 'in the same way as the front of a secretary or desk-drawer'). It is supported on end standards with curved claws and fitted with a boat-shaped shelf below. According to Sheraton, 'the style of finishing them is neat, being commonly made of satin-wood, with a brass moulding round the edge of the rim'. The globe table (Plate 52) is in the Regency style, and this variety is an innovation of that period.

'WRITING FIRE SCREENS'

The 'Lady's Writing Fire Screen' or 'screen desk', although serving somewhat different purposes, was of much the same construction and dimensions as the 'Horse Dressing Glass and Writing Table' (Plate 83), and a very popular article of furniture at the time. Small composite pieces of this form were fashionable in the last two decades of the century. Such desks were often no more than 18 in.

to 2 ft. wide. A fall front enclosed an interior, arranged like that of a writing cabinet, with small drawers and pigeon holes, but very much shallower — the depth of the interior was commonly about 3 in. 'Screen desks' were made either with an open base (the standards being tied by a horizontal stretcher, or a shelf) or were provided with a cupboard below, with flat panelled doors. Shearer contributes two designs for a 'Writing Fire Screen' of this latter sort to the *Book of Prices*. One is intended for the use of 'A Gentleman' and is therefore of more substantial proportions. The plate is dated 1788.

'TAMBOUR OR CYLINDER-FALL WRITING TABLES'

The 'Tambour or Cylinder-Fall Writing Table', again to judge from Shearer's designs for this article in the *Book of Prices*, was clearly a very popular piece, and found useful. Some of these tables are provided with a low arched top or super-structure, containing unenclosed small drawers; and one is fitted with a dressing glass between standards, on a base of two tiers of drawers.

BUREAUX, BUREAU BOOKCASES, LIBRARY CASES AND CABINETS

The term 'bureau', states Sheraton in the *Cabinet Dictionary*, 'has generally been applied to common desks with drawers under them, such as are made very frequently in country towns. They run from 3 to 4 feet long, and have three heights of common drawers under them, the upper one divided into two in length. The desk flap turns down to 30 inches perpendicular height from the ground, or a little less, for sitting to write at.' This piece he describes as 'nearly obsolete in London; at least . . . amongst fashionable people'. The place of the 'common desk' had in fact been taken by the secretary or bureau with 'roll top' or cylinder front and a variety of small cabinets and writing tables (Plates 60, 72, 73).

The bureau in two stages, which in form resembles contemporary bookcases, likewise gave way to the 'Secretary and Bookcase' (Colour Plate A) and the 'Cylinder Desk and Bookcase'. The change is illustrated by Shearer in Plate 7 of the *Book of Prices*. His designs in this instance are not very successful, nor are they wholly representative of work then being done in the shops (Plate 66). Such pieces in the 1780's were commonly made with a straight moulded cornice. Shearer, however, for the 'Secretary and Bookcase' introduces a serpentine cornice (ludicrously decked out with urns or, alternatively, vases, linked by a chain of husks) and for the 'Cylinder Desk and Bookcase', one of arched shape. These members are to be used in conjunction with bookcase doors, with glazing bars arranged in Gothic patterns. The effect is somewhat awkward.

Sheraton's design for 'A Secretary and Bookcase' (Plate XXVIII of the *Drawing Book*) is more characteristic of fashionable production at the end of the century. The design was intended for execution in mahogany, with carved and inlaid decoration, or in satinwood, 'and the ornaments japanned'. The tall proportions of the piece are emphasized by the applied pilasters, framing the doors, and by the straight cornice, surmounted by a lunette-shaped pediment, 'cut in the form of a fan, with leaves in the centre'. The lower stage contains a secretary drawer, letting down on a quadrant, and clothes-press shelves, enclosed by doors, with inlaid oval panels.

The term 'Cylinder Desk and Bookcase' is used by Sheraton also to describe an elegant, lighter piece, mounted on taper legs; the desk of drawers and pigeon holes is enclosed by a tambour front and supports a low upper part of shelves faced by a pair of square doors. A similar article of furniture is illustrated by 'Hepplewhite' in the *Guide*, who refers to it as a 'Tambour Writing Table and Bookcase' (see Plate 74).

The refined appearance of bookcases at this time results partly from their altered proportions (in general there was a reduction in width and an increase in the height of the lower stage) and partly from the considered treatment of the doors (Plates 68, 76). Sheraton devotes great attention to the tracery of the glazing bars, and illustrates in the *Drawing Book* numerous 'patterns for bookcase doors'; his powers of invention were considerable and these patterns are uniformly graceful and very varied, although often embodying attenuated oval forms. He gives also one plate to several 'Pediments for Bookcases' (Plate 25). Large library bookcases were constructed in four and sometimes six compartments, and were break-fronted.

Sheraton's designs for cabinets, both in the *Drawing Book* and the *Cabinet Dictionary*, are distinctive in style and more than usually elaborate. Unlike Hepplewhite, who in the *Guide* does not discriminate between cabinets and bookcases (although a design for a serpentine-fronted cabinet appears under his name in the *Book of Prices*), Sheraton seems here to have allowed his talents free rein. 'The cabinets of gentlemen', he writes in the later publication, 'consist in ancient medals, manuscripts, and drawings, etc. with places fitted up for some natural curiosities. These are the articles of furniture which first gave rise to the general term cabinet making, which has been, from the beginning of this century, considered as one of the leading mechanical professions, in every polite nation in Europe.' Cabinets are, too, 'those curious and neat pieces of furniture, used by ladies, in which to preserve their trinkets, and other curious matters'.[1] He feels with Bacon, who 'thus directs in the furnishing of a favourite room; "at both corners of the further side, let there be two delicate or rich cabinets, daintily paved, richly arranged, glazed with crystaline glass, and a rich cupola in the midst, and all other elegancies that may be thought on" '.

A comparison of two of Sheraton's designs for cabinets, one from the first edition of the *Drawing Book*, the other (from the *Cabinet Dictionary*) in his later Regency style, both for kindred pieces, will illustrate the revolution in taste that had taken place in the closing years of the century (Plates 70, 71) — a change reflected not only in the forms of furniture but in the materials employed (Plates 72, 73).

BOOKSTANDS

The 'moving library, "chiffoniere", or bookstand', an article of furniture introduced late in the century, consisted usually of receding, open shelves for books, above a drawer and sometimes a cupboard; it was supported on stump feet, fitted with castors (Plate 63). One such piece is illustrated in *The Prices of Cabinet Work*, 1797, a publication closely related to the second edition of the *Book of Prices*, but containing additional plates. The various low, light bookcases made at this time were intended 'to contain all the books that may be desired for a sitting room without reference to the library'.

BEDS

The extravagant designs for beds given by Sheraton in the *Drawing Book* are not representative of the output from the shops. It is doubtful if the 'Alcove Bed', the 'Eliptic Bed for a Single Lady' or the 'Summer Bed in Two Compartments' were ever executed. They are fanciful conceptions, having small resemblance to the traditional four-poster, which was plainly constructed (Plates 78, 79), or to the

---

[1] The term 'Cabinet' was applied also to a variety of small writing tables (see pp. 65–66).

lighter, small 'tent' or 'field' bed, with posts about 5 ft. high and curved, rising roof. The four-post bed was expensive mainly because of the importance that was attached to its hangings and 'the high degree of elegance shewn in them'. The amount of materials required in its making was considerable, and, in the late eighteenth century, white dimity, printed cottons and linens, and the 'Manchester stuffs', were more often used than silks, satins and velvets. The cost of the bedstead itself was relatively small. Beds were heavily curtained, often in the same material as was used for the windows of the room. Southey, in the part of Don Espriella, in a 'Description of the Inside, and of the Furniture, of an English House', gives the following account of their furnishing, and of the bedchamber: 'And now', he writes, 'for my own apartment. . . . My bed, though neither covered with silk nor satin, has as much ornament as is suitable; silk or satin would not give that clean appearance which the English always require, and which I have already learnt to delight in. Hence, the damask curtains which were used in the last generation have given place to linens. These are full enough to hang in folds; by day they are gathered round the bed posts, which are light pillars of mahogany supporting a frame work, covered with the same furniture as the curtains; the valances are fastened round this frame, both withinside the curtains and without, and again round the sides of the bedstead. . . . The counterpane is of all English manufactures the least tasteful; it is of white cotton, ornamented with cotton knots, in shapes as graceless as the cut box in a garden. My window curtains are of the same pattern as the bed; a mahogany press holds my clothes, an oval looking-glass swung lengthwise stands on the dressing-table. A compact kind of chest holds the bason, the soap, the tooth brush, and water glass, each in a separate compartment; and a looking-glass for the purpose of shaving at, (for English men usually shave themselves), slips up and down behind, the water-jug and water-bottle stand below, and the whole shuts down a-top and closes in front, like a cabinet [Plate 56]. The room is carpeted; here I have my fire, my table, and my cassette; here I study. . . .'[1]

PRESS BEDS

Press beds, although rarely noticed in the furniture pattern books, had been in use since Stuart times. They were generally constructed to fit into a cupboard or

[1] Southey's *Letters from England*. See footnote 1, p. 61.

'press', or a wardrobe. Hepplewhite, in the *Guide*, illustrates a wardrobe with 'all the appearance of a Press-Bed'; the door, he explains, 'may be made to turn up all in one piece, and form a tester; or may open in the middle, and swing on each side; the under-drawers is useful to hold parts of the bed-furniture.'

The press bed was a plain and useful article of furniture, and one which would be unlikely to reflect current fashions. A sketch for a press bed, supplied by Gillow's in 1789, is here reproduced (Plate 81). It might be judged on stylistic grounds, and on such details as bracket feet, handles and escutcheons, to have been made some ten or fifteen years earlier.

DRESSING TABLES

Various kinds of dressing tables, and dressing and shaving stands, were made at this time (Plates 32, 57B, 80, 83). Shearer, to judge from the numerous designs contained in the *Book of Prices*, would seem to have specialized in this class of furniture. One elaborate piece was that known as a 'Rudd, or Lady's Dressing Table', which was constructed with drawers at the sides which swung out, each fitted with a looking glass rising on a quadrant, and capable of being turned to any position. Hepplewhite refers to Rudd's table as 'the most complete dressing table made, possessing every convenience which can be wanted, or mechanism and ingenuity supply' and states that its name was derived 'from a once popular character, for whom it is reported it was first invented'. Sheraton, submitting a design for a table of this type in the *Drawing Book*, Plate XLVI (Plate 89), is somewhat derogatory and takes credit to himself for his own modifications to it. In the *Cabinet Dictionary*, he refers to Rudd's table as being 'not much in present use' and declares that the advantage it offers, that 'the back part of the head may be seen as well as the front . . . is a mere trifle in comparison to the expence it occasions'.

WASHING STANDS

The wash-stand, designated 'bason-stand' in the trade catalogues, was not introduced as a separate article of furniture until about the middle of the eighteenth century. Most of those surviving from the Sheraton period were made on a triangular plan. Some were fitted with a folding top which served to enclose the basin and, when raised, to screen the wall from water splashes. This variety of basin-stand was desired to 'look neat' and to occupy the corner of a room, where it would be unobtrusive. Sheraton makes the following comments on his designs in the *Drawing Book* for the 'Corner Bason-Stand' (Plate 90A): 'The right-hand bason-stand contains a cupboard and a real drawer below it; by the top folding down the bason is inclosed and hid when it is not in use. The left-hand top is fixed to the side of the bason-stand by a rule-joint, the same as the flap of a Pembroke table; but instead of iron the hinges are made of brass. The right-hand top is hinged to the other by common butt-hinges, by which means it will fold against the other, and both may be turned down together. . . . The bason-stand on the left has a rim round the top, and a tambour door to inclose the whole of the upper part, in which is a small cistern. The lower part has a shelf in the middle, on which stands a vessel to receive the dirty water conveyed by a pipe from the bason. These sort are made large, and the bason being brought close to the front, gives plenty of room. The advantage of this kind of bason-stand is, that they may stand in a genteel room without giving offence to the eye, their appearance being somewhat like a cabinet.' Deception of the kind practised here was quite general, particularly for bedroom furniture since the bedroom was often used as a sitting room. Larger and more elaborate wash-stands were customarily constructed so as to look like a cabinet or small chest-of-drawers.

CHESTS-OF-DRAWERS

The term 'chest-of-drawers' is now used to describe two similar but distinct articles of furniture — sometimes particularized in the late eighteenth century as the 'lobby chest' (or 'chest-of-drawers') and the 'dressing chest'. (The 'tallboy' was also known as a 'chest-of-drawers' or 'chest upon chest'; but Gillow's in their cost books, in 1784, refer to a 'small mahogany Lobby chest or tall-boy' and, clearly, the latter term, too, was current at that time.) Sheraton, in the *Cabinet Dictionary*, distinguishes between the lobby chest, which he defines as 'a kind of half chest of drawers, adapted for the use of a small study, lobby, or small lodging room [bedroom]' and the dressing chest, 'a small case of drawers, containing four drawers in height, the uppermost of which is divided into conveniences for dressing; hence the name dressing-chest'. He gives the main point of difference between the two articles: the dressing chest was constructed with a fitted long drawer at the top (or with a hinged top rising on a quadrant to disclose a glass and fitted well); the lobby chest was not so fitted.

The dressing chest commonly was straight-fronted, about 3 ft. long and 2 ft. 8 in. high and provided with four long drawers, cock beaded round the edges; but its form and dimensions were, of course, variable, according to demand. It was supported on a plinth or on plain bracket feet. Plain 'round-front' (bow-fronted) chests, chests with an 'eliptic sweep' and serpentine-fronted chests were more popular and more costly. They stood usually on bracket or on 'French' feet. Pieces of good quality were provided with numerous extras or refinements; many were veneered on top, front and sides, and cross-banded in kingwood, tulip and other woods; and the dressing drawers were elaborately fitted. The 'standard' lobby chest, with three long and two short drawers above, was larger and of somewhat different proportions, being often 3 ft. 6 in. high.

Sheraton, writing in 1803, recommends smaller pieces and states that lobby chests 'usually consist of four drawers in height, rising to 3 feet in height, and their length about the same. The top drawer is usually divided into two; and sometimes there is a writing slider which draws out under the top. The base and brackets should never be more than 5 inches in height, and the width of the ends 20 inches'. He suggests, likewise, that dressing chests 'if to use standing, may be 3 feet high'. The height of the chest was governed by considerations of use. Persons stood to dress at a lobby chest; they sat, usually, at a dressing chest — unless one constructed with a hinged top. 'But if they sit to dress', remarks Sheraton, 'there must either be a dressing drawer to draw out, or a knee hole in the front when the dressing part is in a well under the top.' The chest then 'must be . . . 32 inches high to the dressing part for sitting'.

Kneehole dressing chests (straight-, bow- and serpentine-fronted) normally contained one long drawer below the top, with three short drawers on either side of the recessed centre, and stood on bracket feet at the six corners. A cupboard was frequently fitted behind the kneehole.

Shearer's designs for chests in the *Book of Prices* include: (i) 'A Serpentine Dressing Chest with straight Wings' and (ii) 'A Serpentine Dressing Chest with ogee Ends' (Plate 90B); and (iii) 'A French Commode Dressing Chest'. Taper stump feet are proposed for the second of the two serpentine-fronted chests, with shelved cupboards at the ends; whereas the French commode chest is shown with 'French' feet and a shaped apron. The forms employed, which are conventional, have been elaborated with some skill.

Two *Drawing Book* designs (Plate 91) for dressing chests are by contrast studiedly elegant. These chests, states Sheraton, are designed 'on a new plan': the shallow top drawer, which contains a little, rising writing flap and 'places for ink, sand and pens, and also dressing boxes', appears when shut 'like a common slider, with a partitition [banding] above and below'. The fronts, framed in one case by reeded pilasters, finishing in decorative stump feet, and, in the other, by engaged half columns, are alternatively of a gentle convex or concave shape. Decorative features of the chests are inlaid panels of contrasting wood, confined and bordered by an ornamental patterning of stringing lines, and cross-banding.

The form of chest with modified bow front, and square corners, was firmly established in popular favour by about 1800. Many specimens were made with a deep frieze below the top, and with shaped apron-pieces (omitted by Sheraton in these designs), used in conjunction with 'French' feet. Alternatively, the reeded, or spiral-twisted, engaged columns frequently to be found on the front corners of such chests terminate in turned feet.

Tallboys, although going out of fashion, continued to be made. Such modifications as were introduced were small and followed those of the plainer sorts of chests.

WARDROBES

The 'common clothes press' was of two tiers: a base, supported on a plinth or on bracket feet, which contained usually two short and one or two long drawers, and an upper part, fitted with four or more shelves for clothes, enclosed by panelled doors (Plates 84, 85). Such pieces were generally made with a straight cornice. Wardrobes, with accommodation for hanging clothes, sometimes with doors opening the full height of the piece, were of much the same character.

Large wardrobes consisted usually of a clothes press flanked by recessed wings. Sheraton describes the composition of these pieces as follows: 'the upper middle part', he states, 'contains six or seven clothes press shelves, generally made about six or seven inches and a half deep, with green baize backed to the inside of the front to cover the doors with. The wings have each of them arms to hang clothes on made of beech with a swivel in their centre which slips on to an iron rod fixed by plates screwed on to each side of the wings.' His design for a wardrobe, given in the *Appendix*, corresponds with this description and, basically, with a plate, dated 1788, published by Shearer in the *Book of Prices* (Plate 67). Sheraton's piece appears the more elegant of the two. It is of taller proportions, and the veneers of the door panels are arranged in a decorative geometrical patterning. The open carved pediment centring in a spray of leaves is of characteristic elliptical form.

MIRRORS

Circular convex mirrors, of a type usually associated with the Regency, were introduced into England towards the close of the century. They had been known in France since the 1750's. They became extremely popular and were, within a few years, 'universally in fashion'. Sheraton, in the *Cabinet Dictionary*, under the heading 'Mirror', disregards other forms. 'As an article in furniture', he writes, 'a mirror is a circular convex glass in a gilt frame, silvered on the concave side.' Convex mirrors produced a distorted and contracted image and appealed by their novelty. As Sheraton observes, 'the perspective of the room in which they are suspended, presents itself on the surface of the mirror, and produces an agreeable effect.' Many such mirrors are surmounted by an eagle with outstretched wings, with acanthus carving at cresting and base (Plate 95), and are provided with candle branches at the sides. There is normally a black-reeded slip fitted between the glass and the gilt frame, which may be of cavetto section with an ornament of small gilt balls, regularly spaced; and the outer mouldings are sometimes reeded and ribboned. Convex mirrors remained in fashion until the 1820's.

Chimney glasses, or overmantel mirrors, in carved gilt frames were designed to rest on the chimney shelf and to extend nearly its length. They were said to 'run various, according to the size of the fire-place, and the height of the wall above' and (1803) to have been 'much in requisition' of late years. They were usually of low, rectangular form and were made, to save expense, with three bevelled plates, divided vertically by thin mouldings, covering the joints. The glass was flanked by pilasters or colonnettes and surmounted by a cornice. There was sometimes an upper panel or broad frieze, decorated in low relief in neo-classical style. The base moulding was narrow, as it was thought 'neatest' to bring the plate as close as possible to the chimney shelf.

Some chimney glasses, however, were of great size, being extended to reach, like pier glasses, 'to the under side of the cornice of the ceiling'. Sheraton states that the pilasters for chimney and pier glasses 'most generally approved' were of

'3, 5, or 7 reeds, worked bold' and recommends for a good appearance their 'being parted with a ground one-third of the width of the reed, which may be matted to relieve the burnished reeds'. He adds that 'it is not unusual to have a twisting branch of flowers, or a ribband round the reeds rising upwards, and terminating in some sort of Composite, Corinthian, or Ionic capital. The pannel above the glass, is sometimes made quite plain, and covered with silk as a ground for drapery, tacked under the cornice of the glass, to match that of the windows'. The design of the frames of these large glasses is generally undistinguished. Some of the most decorative examples were painted (Plate 94).

The two main types of dressing glass in use were the small toilet mirror on a stand and the full-length cheval glass, or 'Psyche'. The design of the former, now in lessened demand owing to the prevalence of fitted dressing tables, which generally contained 'a rising glass', was severe in comparison with the elegantly shaped examples popular in the 1770's and 1780's: the glass, usually oblong, was suspended between turned balusters or tapered uprights, supported on a shallow box stand containing a row of three small drawers. The stand was often straight-fronted or bow-fronted with square corners. Mahogany or rosewood was employed in preference to satinwood, and ornament was restricted to bandings and stringing lines. The stands were sometimes mounted on knobs of ivory or bone, replacing bracket feet, with matching handles and keyhole surround.

Cheval glasses, known as 'Horse Dressing Glasses', were pieces with plates of sufficient size to reflect the whole person; they were rectangular in form. The plate was supported between the two uprights of a standing frame, to which it was attached by means of swivel screws. Sometimes the plate was fixed between the uprights and raised or lowered as needed by weights enclosed within them. Gillow's, in their Estimate and Sketch Books (1799), term the cheval glass 'a screen glass frame'.

POLE SCREENS AND CANDLE STANDS

Pole screens, which Sheraton recommends were to be made of mahogany, or to be painted in white and gold, or japanned, were at this time generally supported on tall, slender, convex- or concave-curving claws, or standards, raised on taper feet (Plates 58, 59). The screen, which was often oval or shield-shaped, was weighted and could be balanced at a touch at the height required; alternatively, adjustment was made by means of a ring and screw. 'Such screens as have very fine prints, or worked satin', says Sheraton, 'commonly have a glass before them.' Panels of needlework, silk embroidery and rolled paper work ('filigree-work') were also in fashion; and gathered silk was popular both for the front of the panel and as a backing.

Sheraton gives three designs in the *Drawing Book* for this type of fire screen. 'The rods', he states, 'are all supposed to have a hole through them, and a pulley let in near the top on which the line passes, and a weight being enclosed in the tassel, the screen is balanced to any height. The rods are often made square, which indeed best suits those which have pulleys, while those that are made round have only rings and springs.'

The standards for tripod candle and flower stands were of a character similar to that of pole screens, but of more stilted proportions (Plate 49). Candle stands were used in drawing rooms 'for the convenience of affording additional light to such parts of the room where it would be neither ornamental nor easy to introduce any other kind'. They were usually gilt, 'finished in white and gold' or 'in inferior drawing rooms . . . japanned answerable to the furniture'.

LONG-CASE CLOCKS

Clock-case making was a specialist craft, even in the country, and was not normally undertaken by the cabinet-maker.

Long-case clocks are remarked by Sheraton in 1803, in the *Cabinet Dictionary*, as 'almost obsolete in London' and no examples are illustrated by him.[1] 'I have given no design of any', he says, 'but intend to do so in my large work [the uncompleted *Encyclopædia*], to serve my country friends.' At this period a notable improvement in provincial clock-making had come about. The cases of provincial clocks were executed in mahogany, which had been increasingly used after about 1760, or, more often, for plainer specimens, in oak, banded with mahogany, fruit wood or satinwood, and inlaid with conventional ornamental *motifs*, such as the fan or shell. By contrast, the cases of some London-made clocks show a clear break with traditional design. The 'regulator' clock illustrated (Plate 65), made with pedestal-shaped body, exemplifies the change.

'Regulator' clocks, which were being extensively made by about 1800, were

[1] He had submitted, however, two designs for a clock case in the *Appendix*.

precision timepieces, designed for accurate time-keeping only; they were furnished with a long 'seconds' pendulum and dead-beat escapement, but were without accessories, such as striking mechanism. The cases of such clocks were generally of excellent workmanship, but plain.

LIBRARY STEPS

Library steps, which came into general use in large private houses after the middle of the eighteenth century, were often disguised or dual-purpose pieces, made sometimes 'to appear like a stool, and at others as a Pembroke table, or to rise out of a library table'. Sheraton, in the *Appendix*, gives two designs for a set of 'Library Steps & Table'. The designs were not his original invention but were reproduced from 'steps that have been made by Mr. Campbell, Upholsterer to the Prince of Wales'. Campbell, who in 1774 had taken out a patent for steps 'to be contained in' tables, 'with or without handrails and with or without desks on the top . . . and in chairs and stools', was prepared to supply these articles to makers for re-sale — although an evasion of the patent rights did not present great difficulty.

There is in the Victoria and Albert Museum a set of steps which resembles the second of those illustrated by Sheraton, and is described as 'not so generally useful' but 'vastly cheaper'. The steps (Plate 36) bear the label of Francis Herve, who, like Campbell, supplied furniture for Carlton House.

COUNTRY AND COTTAGE FURNITURE

There were in most country towns of any size cabinet-makers of good reputation, capable of work which compared favourably with that generally to be bought in London. Specialized craftsmen were employed and Sheraton, who had reason to acknowledge London's predominant position in the trade, observes in the *Cabinet Dictionary*: 'Chair-making is a branch generally confined to itself; as those who professedly work at it, seldom engage to make cabinet furniture. In the country manufactories it is otherwise; yet even these pay some regard to keeping their workmen constantly at the chair, or to the cabinet work. The two branches seem evidently to require different talents in workmen, in order to become proficients.'

London was, of course, the source of new styles and techniques, but the masters of London workshops, who were not compelled to maintain a standard, were free to supply graded goods at widely differing prices (see pages 13, 89). It is probable that little of the furniture made in the last decade of the century was 'in the newest taste'. The design of most pieces of average quality was distinctly conservative. The time lag in fashion, often quite considerable in the provinces, obtained, too, in London.

Provincial makers, aware that the local gentry frequently chose to obtain their furniture in London, attempted to meet competition by such means as lay in their power. This is sufficiently clear from advertisements. Some of these makers were in fact London trained; others employed London workmen or had taken the trouble to acquaint themselves with London fashions. Their goods they commonly declared as 'in the newest taste' and 'as cheap as in London'. Joseph Cooper, a cabinet-maker and joiner of Derby, for example, advertising in the *Derby Mercury* in 1795, informs his public of a change of premises and states that 'he has now begun the Upholstery Trade, for which purpose he has engaged a person from London, duly qualified to execute that business in all its branches, in the best and most complete manner'. And, in the same year, in the *Bury and Norwich Post*, a widow, announcing her intention to carry on her late husband's cabinet business, publicizes her elder son's recent return from London, 'where he has had an opportunity of gaining a thorough knowledge of his employment'.[1] It is not surprising that as many as about 200 of the subscribers to the first edition of the *Drawing Book* were tradesmen drawn from the country.

For the most part, it is difficult to distinguish between furniture made in London and the provinces, despite the persistence, in this, as in earlier periods, of certain features of style, held to be characteristic of different regions.[2]

There are exceptions to the rule that country makers were dependent on town fashions. The 'Mendlesham' chair may be instanced (Plate 14). This variety of chair, sometimes called a 'Dan Day' chair, was made in East Anglia. It has

---

[1] Quoted by R. W. Symonds, *Furniture-making in 17th & 18th century England*, 1955, pp. 130–1.

[2] The North Country chair-maker, for example, favoured heavy, and rather unsightly, stump back legs and a deep seat rail. The rail, which allowed of a larger mortice and tenon joint, strengthened the chair but appeared ungainly and was, therefore, often shaped at the front so as to lighten its appearance. The late R. W. Symonds, who illustrates a shield back chair with these characteristics in the above mentioned work (Fig. 140), remarks the shaped contour of the front rail as a common feature of North Country chairs. The front legs of this specimen are slender and of tapering cylindrical form; and the chair clearly dates from late in the century. Its provincial origin is revealed by the discongruity of the several elements of the design — the light and elegant back and front legs used in combination with sturdy seat frame and back legs.

affinities with the 'Windsor' type, but is distinct from it, particularly in the form of the back, with straight top rail and ball ornaments below. The uprights and rails are often inlaid with boxwood lines, and another characteristic feature is an arched bow at the base of the back. The design is individual and is credited to Daniel Day, a chairmaker and wheelwright of Mendlesham in Suffolk. There exists a tradition that, about 1790, Daniel's son, Richard, worked for Sheraton, afterwards returning to his home.

'What a difference', writes the author of a trades' manual published in 1804, concerned to describe the carpenter's craft, 'is there between the necessary articles of furniture to be found in a cottage, and the elegantly furnished house of a merchant or a peer! In the former there is nothing but what is plain, useful, and almost essential to the convenience of life: in the latter, immense sums are sacrificed to magnificence and show. The cottager is contented with a deal table, an oaken chair, and a beechen bedstead, with other articles equally plain and unexpensive. The wealthy possess sumptuous beds, inlaid tables, silk or damask chairs and curtains, sofas, and carpets of great value; large looking-glasses, and brilliant lustres; together with a variety of carved work and gilding. The furniture of a cottage, or of a small farm-house, will cost but a few guineas; that of a single room in the wealthy parts of the metropolis, will be valued at from five hundred to a thousand pounds.'[1] Much the same might have been said to point a contrast between the furniture of the rich and that of the poor in London and the large provincial towns. In London, as in the country, a considerable quantity of very cheap furniture was sold — 'plain, useful, and almost essential to the convenience of life'. Such furniture (rush-bottomed chairs; tables, desks and chests of wainscot oak) was mass-produced to a common pattern without regard to fashion.

Cottage furniture, however, was made under different conditions. A village carpenter, dealing 'in every sort of work that is made of wood', was, in the words of Adam Smith, 'not only a carpenter, but a joiner, a cabinet-maker, and even a carver in wood, as well as a wheelwright, a plough-wright, a cart and waggon maker.'[2] He was Jack of all trades, and his work, therefore, had some measure of individuality. Cottage furniture does not conform to a standard: its character is local and it is likely to have been made of the native woods readily available in the district of origin.

---

[1] *The Book of Trades or Library of the Useful Arts*, printed for Tabart and Co., London, 1804, Pt. III, pp. 123–5.

[2] Adam Smith, *An Inquiry into the Nature and Causes of the Wealth of Nations*, 1776.

POSTSCRIPT

The designs given by Sheraton in the *Cabinet Dictionary* differ considerably from those of the *Drawing Book*, and the two series, despite their close relationship, are not complementary; indeed, they illustrate styles that are distinct and in many ways antithetical. In the interval of ten years that elapsed between the publication of these two books of designs, there had occurred a complete change of taste, both in England and on the Continent. The *Drawing Book*, which appeared in 1793–4, contained designs which in large part may be taken to represent the last phase of the rectilinear neo-classic style introduced by Adam shortly before 1770. The style was developed until the late years of the century, and was one with which Sheraton had long been familiar.[1] Many of the *Cabinet Dictionary* designs, on the other hand, are in a style now known as 'Regency'. The term is used freely to describe furniture made in the course of the first quarter of the nineteenth century, not necessarily during the period of the Regency of George, Prince of Wales (1811–20). Regency is not a reflection of the personal taste of the Prince Regent, who favoured furniture of the ornate and eccentric kind, as that in the pseudo-Oriental manner supplied for Brighton Pavilion (Plate 17); it is an eclectic style, and complex, which springs from a revived interest, archaeological and doctrinaire in spirit, then becoming widely felt in the remains of the ancient civilizations of Egypt, Greece and Rome (Plates 23, 43). Regency designers, on such evidence as was afforded by material remains in bronze and marble, by reliefs and vase paintings, sought to revive and exactly to copy antique forms. They were prepared to reproduce types of furniture, where precedents existed. (Adam had wished only 'to seize . . . the beautiful spirit of antiquity, and to transfuse it, with novelty and variety'.) Regency has affinity with the current French Empire style. Among its protagonists were Henry Holland, Sir John Soane (Plate 5) and, in particular, Thomas Hope, friend of the French architect and designer, Percier.

Hope, who was trained as an architect and who had studied and travelled in

---

[1] The third, 'revised' edition of the *Drawing Book* was not brought out until 1802, and no essential changes were then made in either text or plates.

Greece and Asia Minor, was himself the owner of a large collection of antiquities. His approach was scholarly, and his designs, published in 1807 under the title *Household Furniture and Interior Decoration*, were made as a record of the work done for his house in Duchess Street, London. They show the style in its purest and most disciplined form.

So much cannot be said for the designs in the *Cabinet Dictionary* (and in the *Encyclopædia*) which precede them (Plates 43, 54, 71, 76). Sheraton did not possess Hope's qualifications; his later work is variable in quality and usefulness, and has, comparatively, little feeling for style. His impressions of the new fashions were gained probably from visits to the shops of London cabinet-makers made in 1802–3, but he would seem then to have been unable to reduce ideas to a satisfactory, reasoned system. He was in failing health and living under wretched conditions. The marked deterioration in his powers may have resulted in part from the fact that his mind was disordered.

The *Cabinet Dictionary* is, however, the first book of designs to record the Regency style. Sheraton submits a number of patterns for the popular 'Grecian' chair (based on the *klismos*), with curved back and sabre-shaped legs; for the 'Grecian' couch, with scrolled ends; for 'curricle', 'Herculanium' and 'X'-framed chairs; for the tripod light and the 'sarcophagus'. He introduces, freely but without discrimination, *motifs* such as the chimera monopodium; dolphin and eagle forms; the hocked animal leg as a support; the archaic lion mask (used frequently as a heading for the legs of chairs) and heavy lion-paw foot. The most striking feature of the designs is the prevalence of curved forms, in particular the adoption of curved supports for chairs and tables.

Surprisingly, Sheraton makes no direct reference in the *Cabinet Dictionary* to the transformed appearance of fashionable furniture at the beginning of the nineteenth century (Plates 9, 15, 47, 52, 55, 95), and abandons without comment his former principles of taste. The following passage, which is to be found under the heading 'Drawing-Room Chairs' throws some light on his state of mind. It is, he says, 'extremely difficult to attain to any thing really novel. If those who expect the purest novelty in such compositions would sit down and make a trial themselves, it would teach them better how to exercise candour when they see designs of this kind'.

NOTES ON THE PLATES

A. Secretary bookcase, with recessed wings, of satinwood, painted and inlaid with various woods (harewood, tulip wood, holly, pear and ebony). The glazed upper stage is surmounted by a scolloped cornice. The central projecting portion of the base contains a deep secretary drawer, with hinged front, above three long drawers. The short taper feet are decorated with inlaid flutes.

Height, 6 ft. 10 in.

c. 1790.

Victoria and Albert Museum.

B. Armchair of painted satinwood, with shield-shaped back and caned seat.

The chair so closely resembles those of a set of seat furniture supplied in 1790 by Seddon's for Hauteville House, Guernsey, as to justify an attribution to this firm. The set is authenticated by a bill; it comprised '18 Sattinwood Elbow Chairs . . . neatly Japann'd — ornamented with roses in back and peacock feather border', a '5 back Settee to correspond' and '3 French Stools' (window seats). Excluding cushions, squabs and carriage charges, these pieces cost respectively 63 guineas (3½ guineas each chair), £17 10s. and £17 6s. 6d. (5½ guineas each 'stool'). Seddon's supplied also on this occasion a very large set of carved mahogany parlour chairs of similar pattern (6 elbow and 26 single chairs) at a cost appreciably lower per chair — the elbow chairs being 57s. each.

Probably by Geo. Seddon, Sons, & Shackleton.

Height, 3 ft. ½ in.

c. 1790.

Victoria and Albert Museum.

C. Side table, of semi-circular form, of painted pine wood; supported on plain taper legs of square section. On the top, an applied oval of parchment, painted in *grisaille* and inscribed 'Lucy Ussher Fecit', enclosed by festoons of flowers painted in colours on a yellow ground, and a floral border. The frieze of the table, painted with a trailing pattern of rose stems, bears the arms of Ussher.

Height, 3 ft.; length, 3 ft. 11 in.

Irish, *c.* 1790.

Victoria and Albert Museum.

D. Commode, of satinwood, with bandings of rosewood and painted decoration of floral bouquets and wreaths. The centre, which is bow-fronted, is flanked by side cupboards of concave outline, framed within pilasters terminating in 'panelled' stump feet.

Height, 2 ft. 10 in.

c. 1790.

Victoria and Albert Museum.

1. 'The Cabinet-maker'.

'His chief tools are, saws, axes, planes, chisels, files, gimlets, turn-screws, hammers, and other tools, which are used in common by the carpenter and the cabinet-maker: but those adapted to the latter are much finer than the tools required by the house-carpenter. The workman represented in the plate is in the act of making a looking-glass frame; he is putting some glue on one of the side-pieces, in order to fix it in the hole that is prepared to receive it.'

From *The Book of Trades or Library of the Useful Arts*, printed for Tabart and Co., London, 1804.

2. Engraved design, frontispiece to *The Cabinet-Makers' London Book of Prices* (editions of 1788, 1793 and 1803), and retained for its successor, *The London Cabinet-Makers' Union Book of Prices* (editions of 1811, 1824, 1836 and 1866). The details of the ornamental border are much as those executed in paint or inlay upon furniture of the period.

3. Design for a mirror; pen and ink and water colour, 6 in. × $2\frac{7}{8}$ in.

Inscribed: 'Thos. Sheraton'.

No other original drawing by Sheraton is known to exist, and the authenticity of this example is not proved. The style of the drawing, however, is consistent with an ascription to Sheraton, who makes use of similar ornamental devices, in particular a distinctive tight foliate scrollwork, in several designs published in the *Drawing Book* and *Appendix*. The winged supporter appears in Plate LVI, dated 1791, entitled 'Ornament for a Frieze or Tablet'.

c. 1790.

Victoria and Albert Museum.

4. One of two engraved views, after drawings by 'T. Sheraton', of Stockton-on-Tees — 'the High Street from the north end of the town'; 23 in. × $14\frac{1}{4}$ in.

The companion view, from the south, measures 20½ in. × 12½ in. and was published by W. Rawson, Bookseller and Printer, Stockton, on 20 February 1785. Sheraton was then in his early thirties.

Public Libraries, Museum and Art Gallery, Stockton-on-Tees.

5. 'The Breakfast Room' at Pitzhanger Manor, Ealing (1802): water-colour drawing by J. M. Gandy.

Sir John Soane's Museum.

Pitzhanger Manor was acquired and rebuilt by Soane in 1800–2 as a country house for his own use. The view shows the original decorations and some of the classical antiquities he had collected.

6. Armchair, of mahogany, supported in front on reeded taper legs of square section, headed by *paterae*; the filling of the square back consists of four carved bars arranged vertically; the curved top rail carved with a trail of husks, and the uprights of the back reeded.

Height, 3 ft. ½ in.

c. 1790–5.

Victoria and Albert Museum.

7. Chair, of mahogany, supported on taper legs of square section; the back is divided into three vertical compartments, the filling incorporating the *motif* of a saltire cross centring in a rosette.

Inscribed in ink on the back of the front seat rail: 'Samuel Fairhead August 1783'.

No maker of this name is recorded; Fairhead does not appear in the contemporary London Directory, or elsewhere. He may have been a journeyman chair maker or, possibly, the original owner of the chair.

For this date, the design of the back is unusual: the chair would seem to be an early example of a type developed by Sheraton in the *Drawing Book*.

Victoria and Albert Museum.

8. One of a pair of chairs, of painted West Indian satinwood, with rounded seat, supported on cylindrical, turned legs. The chair renders, with some modifications, the design given for a 'Drawing Room Chair' in Plate XXXIV of the *Drawing Book*.

c. 1795.

Metropolitan Museum of Art, New York.

9. Armchair, of beech wood, japanned and gilt, with caned back and seat; supported in front on curving legs of baluster form, intersected by rings;

the oval of the back contains a panel painted in *grisaille* with a figure subject; the front rail is decorated with a gilt key pattern (cp. Plate 15.)

Height, 2 ft. 8¾ in.

c. 1800.

Victoria and Albert Museum.

10. Chair, of mahogany, supported on moulded taper legs of square section; the central vase-shaped splat, headed by ostrich plumes, is contained within a compartment, and the uprights of the back are moulded.

The chair back is based on a Hepplewhite design, dated 1787, given in all editions of the *Guide* (the plate might well have formed a model for one included by Sheraton in the *Appendix* to the *Drawing Book*).

'The third edition, improved' (1794) showed a number of new designs which, almost without exception, were for square-backed chairs and sofas in the manner of Sheraton. These designs were presumably incited by Sheraton's gibe (not wholly merited) that the work was outmoded.

c. 1790.

Victoria and Albert Museum.

11. Hall chair, of mahogany, supported on plain, curved legs of square section; the back is vase-shaped and pierced, and carved with festoons of drapery which depend from a broad, moulded top rail, bearing a lunette-shaped piece above. The seat, with sunk centre, is pear-shaped.

Height, 2 ft. 7 in.

c. 1800.

Victoria and Albert Museum.

12. Engraved design for two 'Drawing Room Chairs', dated 1792, by Thomas Sheraton, from the *Drawing Book*, Plate XXXII. The chairs are intended for painting in white and gold, 'or the ornaments may be japanned'.

'The figures in the tablets above the front rails are on French printed silk or satin, sewed on to the stuffing, with borders round them. The seat and back are of the same kind, as is the ornamented tablet at the top of the left-hand chair. The top rail is pannelled out, and a small gold bead mitered round, and the printed silk is pasted on.'

13. One of a set of eight mahogany 'trellis back chairs with stout turned feet to pattern' supplied to Soane by John Robins (Cabinet-maker and Upholsterer of Warwick House, Beak Street, Golden Square) in 1828 for 24 guineas; and one of two armchairs of similar pattern dating from *c.* 1810.

Sir John Soane's Museum.

The set of eight chairs would seem to have been made to match the two armchairs — whose legs are reeded and tapering and not 'stout'. No account exists for the earlier armchairs, but they closely resemble a large set made in 1809 by David Bruce (Cabinet-maker and Upholsterer of 113 Aldersgate Street), under Soane, for the Governor's Room in the Bank of England. These latter chairs were repaired by Robins in 1826. The 'trellis back' pattern derives from late eighteenth-century models, of a type popularly associated with Sheraton; the form of the front legs and of the uprights to the back, however, is consistent with later productions, dating respectively from 1809 and 1828.

14. One of a pair of 'Mendlesham' armchairs, of yew, with solid elm seat; of stick construction, with turned spindle legs.

   Height, 2 ft. 9½ in.; height of seat from floor, 1 ft. 6½ in.; depth of seat, 1 ft. 3 in.

   c. 1800.

15. Armchair, of beech wood, japanned black and gilt, with caned seat; the back painted in colours and *grisaille* with musical instruments, flowers and bands of floral ornament (cp. Plate 9).

   Height, 2 ft. 9 in.

   c. 1800.

   Victoria and Albert Museum.

16. One of a pair of armchairs, of cast iron, with Gothic decoration on a 'Sheraton' frame.

   Early nineteenth century.

   Sir John Soane's Museum.

   Cast iron was employed extensively in the middle and later years of the nineteenth century for garden furniture, hall chairs and hall stands, and the designs were degenerate.

   This is an earlier example of such use of the material.

17. Chair, of imitation bamboo, in the Oriental taste. One of a set of '36 Bamboo chairs japaned; the backs and seats caned' supplied in 1802 by Elward, Marsh and Tatham for the Royal Pavilion, Brighton, for £71; 'Canvas hair cushions for the back and seats covered with red morocco leather' cost the additional sum of £132 6s. 8d.

   Branded, 'G. R. PAVILION'.

Height, 2 ft. 10 in.

Royal Pavilion, Brighton.

18. A, B. Sketch and estimate for 'A Painted chair' made by Gillow's in 1791.

The Gillow Records (Estimate and Sketch Books).

Waring & Gillow, Ltd., Lancaster.

A simple rendering, characterized by the rush seat and the use of stretchers, of a form of chair that was first fashionable about 1780. It is costed at 17s. 6d. — about a quarter or one fifth of the sum required for a fine example, made of satinwood, with painted ornaments (cp. Colour Plate B).

19. A, B. Sketch and estimate for 'A Duchess stuff'd & cov^d wth red leather' supplied by Gillow's to 'Mr Geo. St. Asaph' in 1793. The *duchesse* is composed of two facing, tub-shaped chairs with a stool in the middle. The chairs are detachable (and were costed separately); their framing is exposed and designed 'to shew at the back'. Mahogany was used throughout, therefore, except for the small quantity of white wood (beech) required for the seat rails. The stool part is supported independently at the four corners on square taper legs, with spade feet; and these match the abutting front legs of the chairs. The rail of the stool, however, is not decorated with carved oval *paterae*; and it should be noticed that the engaged sides of the stool are by necessity slightly concave.

The Gillow Records (Estimate and Sketch Books).

Waring & Gillow, Ltd., Lancaster.

20. Settee, of japanned beech wood, with polychrome decoration of floral character; the back, sides and seat caned.

Height, 3 ft. 1 in.; width, 5 ft.

c. 1790–5.

Victoria and Albert Museum.

21. Sofa (*Canapé*), by Georges Jacob (1739–1814); supported on fluted cylindrical legs with acanthus capitals; the cresting of the straight back in the form of a cartouche flanked by sprays of roses; the seat rail with a rosette pattern. The frame is of birch, painted white with carved and gilt ornaments (*réchampi* white and gold). The sofa is upholstered with Beauvais tapestry.

Stamped on the bottom rail at the back: 'G × IACOB'.

Height, 3 ft. 6 in.; width, 5 ft. 9 in.

French, period of Louis XVI.

Wallace Collection.

22. Stool, of mahogany, of rectangular form, supported on turned legs; covered with the original needlework depicting 'King Neptune' and borders of sea-horses.

    Height, 1 ft. 11 in.

    c. 1800.

    Lady Lever Art Gallery.

23. Stool, of mahogany, of 'X' form, with saddle-shaped seat; carved with ram's heads at the extremities of the arms; hoof feet.

    Height of seat, 1 ft. 3 in.

    c. 1805.

    Lady Lever Art Gallery.

    The stool is in the Egyptian taste of the first decade of the nineteenth century. An 'X'-framed construction was common at the time, when designers sought to reproduce forms associated with classical antiquity. Designs for stools of this kind are given in both Thomas Hope's *Household Furniture and Decoration* (1807) and George Smith's *Household Furniture* (1808), and are said by the latter to be 'intended as ornamental and extra seats in elegant Drawing Rooms'. They were generally made of mahogany, or of a soft wood painted, with gilt or bronzed enrichments. A variety with curved seat laid across the upper arms of the 'X'-shaped supports was for use in halls and lobbies.

24. '3 patterns for chair legs': engraved design, dated 1793, by Thomas Sheraton, from the *Accompaniment* to the *Drawing Book*, Plate XIV.

    One of two plates of this character contained in the *Accompaniment*. Sheraton comments that these patterns 'may, in the view of some, be thought too full of work; but the skilful workman will easily see how to reduce their richness, and accomodate them to his purpose'; he explains that 'the centre leg is worked square; that on the right is octagon, except the vase at the knee; and that on the left, round'. His employment of spiral reeding in the last-named example, at this early date, is interesting.

25. Five patterns for 'Pediments for Bookcases': engraved design, dated 1792, by Thomas Sheraton, from the *Drawing Book*, Plate LVII. From the early eighteenth century, several varieties of pediment were employed on case furniture of architectural character. The 'swan-neck' pediment, consisting of opposed 'S' scrolls finishing in *paterae* and flanking an urn or vase raised on a low plinth, was particularly popular. Nos. 1, 3, 4 and 5 are in fact much

modified versions of this form. Segmental, fan- or lunette-shaped pediments, sometimes incorporating a tablet, were very generally adopted towards the close of the century, and are usually made use of by Sheraton in his *Drawing Book* designs.

'The center' of No. 5 'is intended to be veneered and cross-banded, with an oval let in, and japanned. The pedestal above . . . to be thrown back in a hollow carved in leaves'. 'The tablet part' of No. 2 is also suitable for japanning.

26. 'A Plan & Section of a Drawing Room' of a town house: part of an engraved design, dated 1793, by Thomas Sheraton, from the *Drawing Book*, Plate LXI.

In Sheraton's plate, the four walls of the room are shown in elevation. The fourth (short) wall, opposite the fireplace, is here reproduced.

'The commode opposite the fire-place, has four doors; its legs are intended to stand a little clear of the wings; and the top is marble, to match the pier tables. In the freeze part of the commode is a tablet in the center, made of an exquisite composition in imitation of statuary marble. These are to be had, of any figure, or on any subject, at Mr. Wedgewood's, near Soho-square. They are let into the wood, and project a little forward. The commode should be painted to suit the furniture, and the legs and other parts in gold to harmonize with the sofas, tables, and chairs.' Sheraton's design for the room, as he admits, was inspired by Holland's work at Carlton House and Featherstonehaugh House, Whitehall (now Dover House): 'To assist me in what I have here shewn', he writes, 'I had the opportunity of seeing the Prince of Wales's, the Duke of York's, and other noblemen's drawing-rooms. I have not, however, followed any one in particular, but have furnished my ideas from the whole, with such particulars as I thought best suited to give a display of the present taste in fitting up such rooms.'

27. 'A View of the South End of the Prince of Wales's Chinese Drawing Room' in Carlton House: engraved design, dated 1793, by Thomas Sheraton, from the *Appendix* to the *Drawing Book*, Plate XXXI. Of the table Sheraton writes: '. . . the pier table under the glass is richly ornamented in gold. The top is marble, and also the shelf at each end; the back of it is composed of three panels of glass.'

This piece, which is now at Buckingham Palace, was most probably made by Adam Weisweiler, the eminent French master, for Henry Holland, the Prince's architect in charge of the redecoration of Carlton House. Sheraton's reconstruction of the room and its contents, based perhaps on a single visit to Carlton House, is somewhat uncertain.

The table is reproduced by H. Clifford Smith, *Buckingham Palace*, 1931, Fig. 267.

28. A, B. One of a pair of side tables, of broken 'D' shape, supported on turned legs with reeded decoration. The top, veneered with birch, coloured to resemble satinwood, on a mahogany ground, is painted with a central oval containing fruit, flanked by cornucopias filled with flowers springing from musical trophies; the border is painted in a ribbon-and-berry design, enclosed by inlaid strings and a narrow cross-banding of tulipwood. The frieze, carved with a running pattern of leaves and *paterae*, and the legs are gilt. The detachable stand, or shelf, below, is of deal, painted to represent satinwood; the decorative border, reproducing that of the top, is also painted.

Height, 2 ft. 10 in.; length, 4 ft.; depth, 1 ft. 6¾ in.

c. 1790–1800.

Lady Lever Art Gallery.

29. A, B. Side table, carved and gilt, of semi-elliptical form; the top painted primrose yellow and decorated with panels in *grisaille* on a dark brown ground. That in the centre represents the 'Meeting of Bacchus and Ariadne on Naxos' and is based on a painting by Guido Reni in the Palazzo di Monte-citorio, Rome.

The drawers at the sides, with a carved enrichment of laurel sprays, are sham.

One of a pair of tables, of exceptional character, supplied to George, Prince of Wales, for Carlton House, probably to the design of Henry Holland, and later removed to the Royal Pavilion, Brighton.

Stamped at the back: 'G. IV. R. 54.'

Length, 3 ft. 10 in.

c. 1795.

Metropolitan Museum of Art, New York.

The companion table is in the *Victoria and Albert Museum.*

30. Commode, painted, of semi-circular form, supported on turned stump feet; the front, which opens in two side doors, is decorated with oval compartments, surrounded by gilt-composition ribbon mouldings, with figure subjects after Angelica Kauffmann, on a pea-green ground; the stiles and rails ornamented with festoons, *paterae* and wreaths of foliage on a buff-coloured ground.

Height, 3 ft. 6½ in.; width, 3 ft. 8 in.

c. 1790.

Lady Lever Art Gallery.

31. One of a pair of dwarf bookcases, of satinwood, inlaid with tulip and other woods and supported on stump feet.

 c. 1790.

 At Buckingham Palace

32. A, B. Lady's dressing commode of narrow, bow fronted form, veneered with satinwood. The top is painted with an oval of roses and jessamine, flanked by vases containing peacock's feathers, linked by a swag of nasturtiums. The long drawer below, the front painted with a floral festoon, is fitted with a looking glass in a solid satinwood frame, and with boxes, pin cushions and partitions, of unpolished satinwood; the box lids are veneered with burr satinwood and thuya. The two doors of the commode, which are also of satinwood, veneered with satinwood and decorated with painted ovals of classical figures in *grisaille* on a dark green ground, enclose two shelves, constructed of mahogany faced with satinwood. The drawer handles and plates, and the small mounts of the interior, are silver plated. The bandings, bordered by strings, are of tulipwood. The design of this piece is unpretentious, but it is of superb quality.

 Height, 3 ft. 3 in.; length, 2 ft.

 c. 1790.

 Lady Lever Art Gallery.

33. A, B, C. (A) Top of commode, richly inlaid with coloured woods in a ground of harewood. The design radiates from a fan ornament at the back (as was usual in such semi-circular, or semi-elliptical, inlaid surfaces), with leaf tips and pendant husks in boxwood within a *guilloche* border; the field is decorated with a series of festoons of husks (the inlay is shaded), tied by ribbon knots and interrupted by rosette *paterae*; the outer border of meandering honeysuckle or anthemion, in boxwood on a broad band of dark rosewood, is edged by a cross-banding of tulipwood. The rim bears a metal moulding.

 Length, 4 ft. 6½ in.

 c. 1780.

 Lady Lever Art Gallery.

(B) Top of one of a pair of side tables, of satinwood. The design is comparable with that of (A), but is sensitive and more reticent in character. The satinwood veneers are themselves radiated. The beauty of the design owes much to the quality and figure of the wood.

c. 1790.

(C) Top of a commode, which is fitted with drawers in the convex centre, flanked by narrow cupboards, and supported on a low plinth. The radiating design, springing from a conventional fan ornament, closely resembles that of (A), and is adapted very successfully to a shallow top of modified serpentine form.

Length, 3 ft. 6 in.

c. 1790.

34. Pembroke table, of satinwood, with shaped top, cross-banded with mahogany, rosewood, sycamore and boxwood, and fitted with one true and one false drawer. The taper legs are banded to simulate panelling; and the 'therming' of the feet is more than usually graceful.

Originally the property of Mrs. Fitzherbert, at Brighton.

c. 1790.

Royal Pavilion, Brighton.

35. Tea table, of inlaid satinwood, of circular form, supported on three curved legs united by a collar. A panel of black and gold Japanese lacquer is inset in the top, which is bordered with mahogany. The rim is inlaid with kingwood and other woods.

Diameter, 2 ft. 10 in.

c. 1795–1800.

At Buckingham Palace

36. A, B. Library steps, of mahogany, made to fold into the drawer of a small table, and enclosed by a hinged flap, with three solid treads attached.

The piece closed.

Bearing the inscribed label of Francis Hervé, of 32 Lower John Street, Tottenham Court Road, active *c.* 1785–96.

The steps closely resemble the plainer of two designs illustrated in the *Appendix* to the *Drawing Book*, for which Sheraton acknowledges indebtedness to 'Mr. Campbell, Upholsterer to the Prince of Wales', the patentee (see page 39).

c. 1790.

Victoria and Albert Museum.

37. A, B, C, D. Oval breakfast table, of mahogany, with a border of tulipwood, cross-banded and enclosed by strings; on a 'pillar-and-claw' support.

Three 'pillar-and-claw' parts, of a type used variously for dining, breakfast and loo tables, and for circular, drum-topped library tables.

c. 1795–1800.

38. Engraved design for 'A Universal Table', dated 1791, by Thomas Sheraton, from the *Drawing Book*, Plate XXV. The table is extended by means of draw leaves, and fitted with raking sliders. 'When both the leaves are slipped under the bed', writes Sheraton, 'it will then serve as a breakfast-table; when one leaf is out, as in this view, it will accommodate five persons as a dining-table; and if both are out, it will admit of eight, being near seven feet long, and three feet six inches in width.' The drawer, divided into boxes at each side, 'for different sorts of tea and sugar, and sometimes for notes, or the like', is double-fronted, and pulls out both ways. Sheraton observes that much depends on the table's being made of good, well-seasoned mahogany, that is not 'liable to cast'. Preferably, 'the tops are framed and pannelled; the bed into two pannels, and the flaps each into one, with a white string round each pannel to hide the joint. The framing is three inches broad, and mitered at the corners; and the pannels are sometimes glued up in three thicknesses, the middle piece being laid with the grain across, and the other two lengthways of the pannel, to prevent its warping. The pannels are, however, often put in of solid stuff, without this kind of gluing.'

39. Engraved design for 'A Library Table', dated 1791, by Thomas Sheraton, from the *Drawing Book*, Plate XXX.

'The style of finishing it ought to be in the medium of that which may be termed plain or grand, as neither suits their situation. Mahogany is the most suitable wood, and the ornaments should be carved or inlaid, what little there is; japanned ornaments are not suitable, as these tables frequently meet with a little harsh usage. The strength, solidity, and effect of brass mouldings are very suitable to such a design, when expence is no object. For instance, the pilasters might be a little sunk, or pannelled out, and brass beads mitered round in a margin, and solid flutes of the same metal let in. The astragal which separates the upper and lower parts might be of brass; and likewise the edge of the top, together with the patera in the upper pannel, as shewn on the left hand. The top is lined with leather or green cloth, and the whole rests and is moved on castors hid by the plinth.'

40. A, B. (A) Semi-circular cellaret sideboard, of finely figured mahogany, inlaid and decorated with a minute marquetry of Tunbridge-ware character; the

shallow centre drawer is angled and is flanked, on the left, by two drawers and, on the right, by one deep drawer (panelled to represent two), fitted with divisions for bottles; the end cupboards also are angled. The taper legs, inlaid with floral *paterae* on a boxwood ground and with pendant husks, are not of square section, but are 'bevelled' at the sides so as to conform with the side rails of drawers and cupboards. The spandrels to the arch below the centre are inlaid with a fan decoration. The circular handles and plates are original.

Length, 5 ft. 2 in.

c. 1790.

Lady Lever Art Gallery.

This piece closely resembles a design, dated 1788, by Shearer, contributed to *The Cabinet-Makers' London Book of Prices*, 2nd ed., 1793, Plate 5, Fig. 1, (Plate 41) but is provided with two 'extra legs in front' and with 'two drawers in place of a deep one', on the left. There are also various decorative refinements, notably 'extra work in arch'.

(B) Bow-fronted cellaret sideboard, of mahogany, with an inlay of ebonized stringing lines; supported on plain taper legs, 'bevelled' at the sides (as in preceding specimen) and finishing in moulded feet.

Length, 5 ft. 6 in.

c. 1795.

Victoria and Albert Museum.

41. Two engraved designs, dated 1788, for a cellaret sideboard, by Thomas Shearer, from *The Cabinet-Makers' London Book of Prices*, 2nd ed., 1793, Plate 5:

Fig. 1. 'A Circular Celleret Sideboard' — 'Five feet long, the framing fifteen inches deep, two deep drawers, one prepared for the plumber, the other plain, a shallow angle ditto in the middle, a cupboard in each corner, veneer'd front . . . Marlbro' legs, and an astragal round the bottom of the frame.'

Fig. 2. 'A Celleret Sideboard, with Eliptic Middle' and, alternatively, an 'Ogee' or an 'Eliptic Hollow' on each side.

42. Engraved design for 'A Side Board', dated 1792, by Thomas Sheraton, from the *Drawing Book*, Plate XXVI (plate marked '54' in error).

Sheraton remarks that the left-hand drawer is 'sometimes made very short, to give place to a pot-cupboard behind, which opens by a door at the end of the sideboard. This door is made to hide itself in the end rail as much as possible, both for look and secrecy. For which reason a turn-buckle is not used, but a thumb-spring, which catches at the bottom of the door, and has a communication through the rail, so that by a touch of the finger the door flies open, owing to the resistance of a common spring fixed to the rabbet which the door falls against.' The mechanism is illustrated in the diagram inset.

43. Engraved design for a 'Grecian Dining Table', by Thomas Sheraton, from the *Cabinet Dictionary*, 1803, Plate 47 (48 in the index). Sheraton's later designs in imitation of the antique often appear forced, and the above is no exception. The table, which is shaped as a horseshoe, is composed in three parts, each with two flaps, letting down 'as those of a pembroke table', each being 6 ft. long and 2 ft. 6 in. wide; they are joined by brass trap fasteners on the undersides. The table is narrow and designed to seat, on the outer side only, nine persons. Sheraton claims that the shape is well adapted for the purpose of dining 'in admitting a dumb waiter in the centre' of the hollow side, with ample room also for two servants — who have, therefore, 'very easy access to the table'. There is the convenience that the parts may be used separately as sofa tables — 'if the hollow side [of each table] be turned to the front of a sofa' and, he says, 'there be one or two drawers introduced, which may easily be done.' The table, couches and dumb waiter shown in the plate are *en suite*, with common features in curved, sabre-shaped legs, ringed lion masks and fret pattern ornament. 'In the back ground is a suitable side-board, supported with antique figures, over which, on the top, are placed two female ones, holding lights.'

44. Engraved design for 'A Kidney Table', dated 1792, by Thomas Sheraton, from the *Drawing Book*, Plate LVIII.

'The drawers which appear in the design are all real, and are strung and cross-banded, with the grain of the mahogany laid up and down. The pilasters are pannelled or cross-banded, and the feet below turned. The view of it below shews the ends pannelled, and the back may be so too, or it may be plain.'

45. Engraved designs for 'A Gentleman's Social Table' and 'A Knee-Hole Kidney Library Writing Table', dated 1792, by 'Heppelwhite', from *The Cabinet-Makers' London Book of Prices*, 2nd ed., 1793, Plate 22, Figs. 1 and 2.

The social, or wine, table is described as follows: 'Four feet long, the rail two inches and a half wide, veneer'd all round, solid top, square edge to ditto, four plain taper legs, a pillar and claw stand in the hollow part, the top of ditto turn'd to receive the bottom of a tin or copper cylinder, two feet over and made to turn round, a mahogany top fitted into the cylinder, and cut to receive five tin bottle cases.'

46. 'Carlton House' writing table, of mahogany, supported on plain taper legs of square section. The table is fitted with a rising desk; there are three drawers in the frame, and various small drawers and compartments in the super-structure, with curved ramps at the ends. The piece corresponds closely with a design by 'Hepplewhite' for 'A Gentleman's Writing Table', dated 1792, which appears in *The Cabinet-Makers' London Book of Prices*, 2nd ed., Plate 21.

 c. 1795.

47. Circular library table, of rosewood, partly gilded and inlaid with satinwood; the revolving top covered with leather. The books between the drawers in the frieze are dummy. The table is supported on a central pedestal, with four carved and inlaid 'claws', finishing in brass toes.

 Diameter, 4 ft. 6 in.

 c. 1800.

48. Sixteen patterns for 'thermed' legs, dated 1792, by William Casement, from *The Cabinet-Makers' London Book of Prices*, 2nd ed., 1793, Plate 28.

 The patterns were to be applied to stump feet and legs of various sizes: (i) cellaret legs; (ii) card, Pembroke and work table legs; (iii) dining, sideboard and pier table legs. Nos. 1–6 are for 'Marlbro'' legs, that is, taper legs of square section; nos. 7–16, for legs of round section. The patterns are ordered numerically by price — no. 1 being the cheapest (4d.–7d. each leg, according to type and size), no. 16, the dearest (1s. 5d.–1s. 8d.).

 'Therming in the Neck', which was suitable for nos. 1–6, was an extra charge, ranging from 3d.–1s. 3d.

 The taper leg of square section was, of course, often made plain, without a 'thermed foot'. 'When the legs are therm'd at the top only, the tapering to be paid for extra.'

49. Various patterns for 'claws', 'standards', etc., dated 1793, by 'Hepplewhite', from *The Cabinet-Makers' London Book of Prices*, 2nd ed., 1793, Plate 29.

 The 'claws' (12 patterns) are suitable for (i) 'horse' fire screens and music stands; (ii) screen desks and dressing glasses; (iii) dining or loo tables.

 Nos. 1–9 are of square section, nos. 10–12, round. The feet of nos. 1–4 are suitable for 'therming' (6 patterns). The standards for tripod fire screens (9 patterns), with the exception of no. 7, and the taller standards for flower and candle stands (4 patterns) are of square section, and might appropriately be moulded, 'panelled' or ornamented with strings. There are shown also mouldings for case furniture and the working detail of alternative 'falls' for a cylinder writing table.

50. Lady's work table (pouch variety), of satinwood, with mahogany stringing lines.

The table is fitted at the back with a sliding fire screen. The work bag, or pouch, which is of silk, is attached to a satinwood frame which pulls out to one side; on the other is a drawer, fitted with small compartments for writing. There is a slide at either end of the table below the adjustable leather-covered top. The frieze is in the form of a false drawer with circular brass ring handles.

This piece has some resemblance in form and proportions to Sheraton's design for 'A Reading & Writing Table', the *Drawing Book*, Plate XLIV (Plate 57A).

Height, 2 ft. 6 in.; width, 1 ft. 8 in.

c. 1790.

Victoria and Albert Museum.

51. Work table of the '*tricoteuse*' type, of satinwood, with inlaid trellis decoration of rosewood and satinwood; the lyre-shaped supports united by an oval platform.

Inlaid ornament of much this character and pattern occurs on a work table ('*tricoteuse*' or '*vuide poche*') made by A. Weisweiler, which is in the Wallace Collection (F. 325). See F. J. B. Watson's *Wallace Collection: Catalogue of Furniture*, 1956, Plate 77.

Width, 2 ft. 4 in.; depth, 1 ft. 2 in.

c. 1795.

52. Work table, of mahogany, in the form of a globe on stand, the quarters being divided by fine stringing lines of holly meeting at the top in a brass *patera*.

The curved legs of square section, headed by brass lion masks with rings, are united below by a galleried bowl to contain the odds and ends of needlework. The top drops back to disclose a recessed temple niche, backed by panels of looking glass, with columns in front and chequered parquet floor; the front half fitted in compartments with numerous small drawers and receptacles for work.

Height 3 ft.

c. 1805–10.

Lady Lever Art Gallery.

A similar table, bought by Queen Charlotte as a birthday gift for the Princess Augusta in 1810, is at Buckingham Palace, and is illustrated in M. Jourdain's *Regency Furniture*, revised edition 1949, Figs. 120–1.

53. Terrestrial globe, supported on a mahogany stand, with reeded legs tied by turned stretchers centring in a small circular platform.

The globe, which is one of a pair (terrestrial and celestial), by W. and T. M. Bardin, and dated 1843.

Height of stand, 2 ft.

c. 1800.

Victoria and Albert Museum.

54. Nest, or 'quartetto', of tables, of satinwood, feather-banded with tulipwood with ebony cock beading and inlay. The piece corresponds with a design by Sheraton, dated 1803, for a 'Quartetto Table' ('a kind of small work table made to draw out of each other, and may be used separately, and again inclosed within each other when not wanted') in the *Cabinet Dictionary*, Plate 75 (78 in the text).

Height, 2 ft. 4 in.

c. 1805.

Southey, in his *Letters from England*, refers to 'a nest of tables for the ladies, consisting of four, one less than another, and each fitting into the one above it'. 'You would take them for play-things', he says, 'from their slenderness and size, if you did not see how useful they find them for their work.' George Smith (*Household Furniture*, 1808) states that such tables were placed in the drawing room, where they 'prevent the company rising from their seats, when taking refreshments'.

A set of three tables was known as a 'trio-table'.

55. Drum-top table, of rosewood, on tripod stand; the curved 'claws' rest on castors and are united by a plain platform. Ornament has been kept to a minimum (the front surfaces of the 'claws', for example, are without strings) and the maker has relied for effect on the decorative appearance of rosewood used with brass, and on the graceful form and proportions of the table.

c. 1800.

Thomas-Stanford Museum, Brighton.

56. Engraved designs for 'A Music Stand', 'A Lady's Work Table', 'A Travelling Bidet' and 'A Shaving Stand', dated 1792, by 'Hepplewhite', from *The Cabinet-Makers' London Book of Prices*, 2nd ed., 1793, Plate 25, Figs. 1–4.

These articles are described as follows:

The music or reading stand — 'The top one foot eight inches long, one foot two inches wide, an astragal on the edge of ditto, a fram'd bottom fix'd to the pillar, a hollow on the edge of the framing, a horse to support the top, and three claws.'

The work table — 'One foot six inches long, one foot two inches wide, framing four inches deep, one drawer in ditto, cock beaded, plain taper legs, the top part eight inches and a half wide, and eight inches deep, made to take off, one long and two short drawers in ditto, and a plain tray top.' As shown in the plate it is made with various extras, including an ornamental stretcher; the legs are 'sprung both ways' and the back of the upper part is 'scollop'd'.

The bidet — 'To rise out of a chest, the top hung with slip hinges, the inner ends fram'd flush with the feet inside, the outer ends to fly out with springs to support the bidet when up, two grooves in each end, a pin through each foot to slide in the groove and stop the bidet in, the edge of the top moulded, and a plinth round the bottom.'

The shaving stand — 'One foot seven inches at the back, one foot six inches from back to front, framing one foot four inches deep, one real drawer, one sham ditto, and a plain door in front, a flap top, with an astragal on the edge of ditto, a glass frame to rise with a rack and spring, four plain Marlbro' legs, or the cants continued down and cut to form the legs, the cants either solid or veneer'd.' The stand is shown with 'canted corners' (left) or, alternatively, with 'hollow corners' (right).

57. A, B. (A) Engraved designs for 'A Reading & Writing Table' and 'A Writing Table', dated 1792, by Thomas Sheraton, from the *Drawing Book*, Plate XLIV.

(B) Engraved designs for a cylinder-fall wash-hand dressing chest, fitted with rising glass frame, cistern and night stool and 'A Lady's Cabinet', dated 1792, by 'Hepplewhite', from *The Cabinet-Makers' London Book of Prices*, 2nd ed., 1793, Plate 23.

The cabinet is to be 'Two feet six inches long, one foot six inches from front to back, framing four inches deep, one drawer in ditto, cock beaded, a flap nine inches wide hing'd to the front with card-table hinges, supported by two lopers to draw out at the top of the legs, a case on the back part nine inches wide and nine inches high, a cupboard at each end, plain doors to ditto, the center part open, flat top, plain taper legs, and an astragal round the bottom of the frame'. In the plate the piece is shown with the top 'made serpentine' and the doors of the 'case' veneered — both extras.

58, 59. Sketch and estimate for 'A satin wood Japan'd tripod fire screen: the fluted pillar as usual ommited', made by Gillow's in 1791.

    The Gillow Records (Estimate and Sketch Books).

    Waring & Gillow, Ltd., Lancaster.

60. Lady's cylinder desk, veneered with rosewood and satinwood. There is no superstructure, but the top of the desk is fitted with a brass gallery at back and sides. The piece is of very small proportions. The combination of woods is a little unusual and shows most effectively in the 'panelling' of the legs. The 'cylinder fall' and 'slider' act interdependently.

    Width, 2 ft.

    c. 1800.

61. Lady's writing table, made by Gillow's; of satinwood, banded with king-wood, with inlaid strings of ebony and boxwood. The low superstructure is fitted with two tiers of small drawers and eight pigeon holes. The table has a hinged turn-over flap supported on lopers (draw runners). It is made of carefully chosen woods and may be regarded as representative of the firm's best production; it is unpretentious, simply constructed and conservative in style (see page 36). This piece of furniture, termed often by contemporaries a 'Lady's Cabinet', corresponds quite closely with a design by 'Hepplewhite', in *The Cabinet-Makers' London Book of Prices* (Plate 57B), although there is some difference in size and in the form of the 'case'. Its shape and proportions are modelled on the French 'Bonheur du jour', of which painted varieties were also fashionable in this country.

    Stamped 'GILLOWS LANCASTER' on the top of the drawer front.

    Width, 2 ft. 3 in.

    c. 1790–1800.

62. Lady's cabinet on stand, of mahogany. The exterior and interior surfaces are painted with figures and various ornamental *motifs* (mostly floral) on a pale straw-coloured ground. The dominant feature of the decoration is the painting of the door fronts — a pair of oval panels, in full colour, one representing 'Venus with Cupid in a chariot', the other, 'Nymphs sacrificing before an altar over which Cupid hovers'; the enclosing spandrels are 'marbled' in dark green. The inside of the doors, which open to disclose an interior of eleven small drawers, made of cedar wood, is executed in monochrome with

classical figures in ovals on a blue background. The cabinet is bow fronted and of very small proportions. Its appearance, when closed, is strikingly colourful. The painting, nevertheless, is inferior in execution to the cabinet work: many such pieces, said to have been decorated by Angelica Kauffmann or by Cipriani, were in fact by lesser hands — by copyists from the popular engravings of their works published by Boydell and others.

The cabinet is stated to have been at one time the property of James Hook, the composer (1746–1827), for many years organist at Vauxhall Gardens. His songs include 'Within a Mile' and 'The Lass of Richmond Hill'.

Height, 4 ft.

c. 1790.

Lady Lever Art Gallery.

63. Bookstand, or small cabinet, with cupboard base. The piece is executed in satinwood, with inlaid panels and stringing lines in ebony and boxwood; the cupboard door decorated with an oval panel of finely figured mahogany; the taper stump feet 'panelled' and elaborately formed. The open shelves of the upper part are surmounted by a brass gallery.

Height, 3 ft. 9 in.; width, 1 ft. 9 in.; depth, 11 in.

c. 1795.

64. 'A Lady's Writing Table'.

The piece is based on a design, dated 1792, illustrated by Sheraton in the *Drawing Book*, Plate XXXVII, but is likely to date from the first years of the nineteenth century, since it is executed in rosewood, with brass mounts, and the geometrical patterning of the ornamental stringing lines is markedly severe. The maker had access, perhaps, to the third edition of the *Drawing Book* (1802). As envisaged by Sheraton, the table was to be made 'of satinwood, cross-banded' and finished 'neat, and rather elegant', with painted ornaments of swags of drapery and husks, and formalized flowers; there was provision for a screen at the back of the table, raised by a system of concealed pulleys and weights and seated on a low shelf or platform, with concave front deeply recessed so as to afford leg room to the user. 'The convenience of this table is', remarks Sheraton, 'that a lady, when writing at it, may both receive the benefit of the fire, and have her face screened from its scorching heat.' In essentials, however, the correspondence between the table as executed and the design is close, and the proportions are much the same. The legs are tapered and of square section — and it is of interest that the maker chose to retain this conservative feature. The small drawers for writing materials, which are contained in the stepped side-boxes, are released by pressure on protruding *paterae* 'and fly out of themselves, by force of a common spring'. At the sides of the writing drawer are small enamel plaques.

c. 1805.

65. Balloon long-case clock, in a case veneered with mahogany, with brass ornaments; simulating a balloon-cased bracket clock supported on a term, or pedestal.

The 'regulator' movement by Thomas Iles, London.

c. 1795.

66. Two designs for a bureau bookcase, dated 1788, by Thomas Shearer, from *The Cabinet-Makers' London Book of Prices*, 2nd ed., 1793, Plate 7.

The 'Secretary and Bookcase' (left) is made with a deep secretary drawer, with cupboard doors below, and supported on either ogee or plain bracket feet; the 'Cylinder Desk and Bookcase' (right), with a sliding cylinder or tambour front, delicate outward-pointing feet and shaped apron. The four 'patterns for doors' are of Gothic character.

Shearer's adoption here of a shaped cornice is unsuccessful; neither of the designs is satisfactory.

67. Engraved design, dated 1788, for a wardrobe, by Thomas Shearer, from *The Cabinet-Makers' London Book of Prices*, 2nd ed., 1793, Plate 3:

'A Wing Clothes Press' — 'Six feet eight inches long, six feet nine inches high to the top of the cornice, two flat-pannel'd doors to the upper carcase of middle part, pannels plow'd in, six clothes shelves inside ditto, two long and two short drawers in the lower part, cock beaded, the wing doors to open from top to bottom, with two pannels in each, plow'd in, four fast shelves inside one wing, turn'd pegs in the other, loose cornice, fram'd backs to the top and bottom of middle part, fast plinth.'

The many, various 'extras' include: veneering the drawer fronts, the panels of the doors, the ends of the piece, etc.; supplying sham or real drawers in the lower part of the wings; and making with pilasters on the stiles of the wing doors. Some of the improvements are embodied in the specimen design. The alternative forms recommended for the piece are also shown.

68. Bookcase, of mahogany, of tall and elegant proportions; the glazed upper stage surmounted by a fan-shaped pediment, with inlaid decoration; the base, enclosed by a pair of doors, rests on a plain plinth.

The piece is representative of the refined taste of the closing years of the century, and depends for effect on the rich figure of the selected veneers and fine quality of the workmanship.

c. 1795.

69. China cabinet, of satinwood; the upper part with glazed doors of 'Gothic' character, and 'Gothic' cornice; the base, with kneehole in the centre, supported on short 'panelled' taper legs.

The cabinet, particularly its front (enriched by the mottled figure of the veneers, with fine bandings and an ornament of strings) is extremely decorative; the execution is of very high standard.

The beading above the 'Gothic' drops of the cornice is stopped at the sides, which are comparatively plain, with an ornament of ebony strings.

Height, 7 ft. 3 in.; width, 2 ft. 10 in.; depth, 1 ft. 6 in.

c. 1790.

70. Engraved design for 'A Cabinet', by Thomas Sheraton, from the *Drawing Book*, Plate XLVIII.

'The use of this piece is to accommodate a lady with conveniences for writing, reading, and holding her trinkets, and other articles of that kind.' The silk and drapery in the centre door of the upper part conceal sliding shelves for small books. The drawer above the kneehole is fitted with a writing slide, while those on each side are plain. 'The style of finishing' such cabinets, observes Sheraton, 'is elegant, being often richly japanned, and veneered with the finest satin-wood.'

71. Engraved design for 'An elegant cabinet for a lady', dated 1802, by Thomas Sheraton, from the *Cabinet Dictionary*, 1803, Plate 26A (26 in the index, 24 in the text).

'If the cabinet be of black rose wood', states Sheraton in the explanatory notes, 'the columns or legs . . . ought to be carved and gilt. The open wings of the upper part may be either cut out in wood glued up in thicknesses, in the manner of the fret work formerly used, or may be cast in brass. The tray tops . . . ought decidedly to be in brass, both for strength and beauty . . . The ornament at the top of the framing of both lower and upper doors is intended to be a part of the framing, to be cut out in a light manner, and gilt, which will suit the wire work before the silk.' He remarks also that the 'round ends of the lower part may be either formed of solid doors, veneered, and banded, or of wire and silk, as those in the hollow of the front'. Rosewood was freely employed in the first decade of the nineteenth century, to a great extent supplanting satinwood. The cost of labour and materials had risen steeply as a result of the French war. Inlaying had become a 'very expensive mode' of decorating furniture; cabinet-makers relied for effect instead on the contrast obtained by using dark woods in combination with inlays and/or mounts of brass (see also Plate 64).

72. Lady's writing cabinet, of satinwood, elaborately inlaid with various woods, and ornamented with *ormolu* mounts. The semi-circular front of the base is divided by pilasters and a horizontal *ormolu* beading into six main panels. The centre contains three long drawers (their fronts inlaid as a single decorative unit) below a writing compartment consisting of pigeon holes, shallow drawers and small cupboard, enclosed by sliding panels, and which may be drawn forward for use. In the superstructure a small cupboard in the centre, with two folding doors, is flanked by two tiers of four drawers with serpentine fronts, and there are end cupboards. The scroll-work rail at each end of the top shelf is of *ormolu*, as is also the finial surmounting the cabinet.

    c. 1795.

73. Lady's writing cabinet, in two tiers.

    The upper part is formed in three cupboards, veneered with satinwood and decorated with painted panels of bouquets of flowers on a grey ground; the sides surmounted by a mahogany spindle gallery, the centre by a shallow pediment of segmental form. The base centres in a small cylinder top desk, which opens automatically when the drawer below, fitted with a rising shelf for writing, supported on a ratchet, is pulled out; the interior has two small cupboards, the doors of which are ornamented with Wedgwood plaques, four shallow drawers and a well for papers. Beneath the desk is a deep cupboard, with concave door covered with pleated silk. The tall cupboards at the sides, contained within slender pilasters, are convex and are veneered with satinwood, framing panels of sacquebu (a dark, contrasting wood, similar in appearance to some growths of mahogany and rosewood). The interior of the cabinet is of mahogany, and the back panelled. The workmanship is of the highest quality.

    Height, 5 ft. 6 in.

    c. 1795.

    Lady Lever Art Gallery.

The cabinet does not correspond closely with any of Sheraton's published designs but is characteristic of his style at the time (see Plate 70 and pages 29–30).

74. Bureau cabinet, of yew; the upper part with glazed doors of 'Gothic' character, and 'Gothic' cornice, beneath a scrolled pediment; the base supported on taper legs of square section, cross-banded with kingwood. The cylinder fall of the bureau, enclosing a finely fitted interior, is actuated by the drawer in the frieze.

    c. 1785.

75. Cabinet, veneered with sacquebu and East Indian satinwood. The pediment centres in a clock, which bears the name 'Weekes Museum, Tichborne Street'. The upper drawer of the lower stage of the cabinet is fitted with numerous small boxes and covers, with silver mounts, and a rising mirror; below, is a secretary drawer, with fall front, and a cupboard enclosed by panelled doors, which contained originally a musical box, actuated by the clock and playing at the hours and quarters. (Mechanical clocks and toys, and various musical boxes, were included in the collection at the Weekes Museum, which was one of the places of amusement in the Haymarket in the late eighteenth century.)

    A similar cabinet, presumably by the same maker, is illustrated in *The Dictionary of English Furniture* (revised edition by Ralph Edwards, 1954, Vol. I, 'Cabinets', Fig. 71). This latter piece more closely resembles one reproduced by P. Macquoid (*The Age of Satinwood*, 1923, Fig. 187), which is stated to have been 'originally one of a set of three pieces, the largest being headed by a clock, the other two with round Wedgwood plaques'. A cabinet at the Lady Lever Art Gallery is also executed in satinwood and sacquebu (Plate 73).

    c. 1795.

    City Museum and Art Gallery, Birmingham.

76. 'A cylinder bookcase with wings'; the finely figured mahogany veneers on the cupboard doors and drawer fronts of the lower stage decorated with strings; the compartments framed by reeded pilasters.

    The bookcase corresponds closely with a design illustrated by Sheraton in the *Cabinet Dictionary*, 1803, Plate 39: 'I took the idea of it', writes Sheraton, 'from one I have seen executed by Mr. John Somerville, Chancery-Lane, and if it be a little improved, that is all I claim in this piece. The cylinder rises from the front upwards, and there is a slider to come forward as usual. . . .

The lower wings are here divided into two parts, the upper for cupboards and the right hand lower part into plain drawers, and left open as a closet.'

c. 1803.

77. Chamber organ; the case of mahogany, satinwood and rosewood, with inlaid decoration and cross-banding. By James Hancock, 'organ builder to His Majesty'; dated 1788.

Until recently, the organ had been stored for many years in the tower of the Roman Catholic Church of St. Mary, Brighton. In view of this history and of the instrument's having been constructed by a maker to the Crown in 1788, it has been suggested that it may have belonged originally to Mrs. Fitzherbert's Brighton house.

Royal Pavilion, Brighton.

78, 79. Sketch and estimate for 'A mahog. Bedstead wth reeded pillars' supplied by Gillow's in 1793.

The posts are cylindrical and reeded, tapering upwards from a 3 ft. pedestal of square section to the 'sweep' of the tester — not, as was more usual at the time, from a slender vase-shaped form and low pedestal. Individual workmen were engaged on the 'making', 'turning', 'painting' and 'varnishing'. The headboard is stuffed.

Height, about 13 ft.

The Gillow Records (Estimate and Sketch Books).

Waring & Gillow, Ltd., Lancaster.

80. A, B. Sketch and estimate for 'A white wood Japan'd dressing table' supplied by Gillow's to 'Robert Watkin Wynn Esqre' in 1793.

The Gillow Records (Estimate and Sketch Books).

Waring & Gillow, Ltd., Lancaster.

The table is costed at £2 10s. 8d. and occupied an employee, Robert Fell, some ten days in the making. It is elegantly proportioned but it is not distinguished by any newly fashionable features and might well be thought to date from the 1780's: it is straight-fronted, constructed with a box lid enclosing fitted compartments and looking glass, and is supported on plain taper legs. Dressing tables of this form, however, and sturdy and more compact specimens, fitted with cupboard and drawers, which were called 'Shaving Tables', retained popularity throughout the later years of the century. One of the several varieties of dressing tables illustrated in the *Drawing Book* is of this pattern.

Gillow's production, in general, must have resembled that of many other makers, both London and provincial, although their position in the trade was unusual, inasmuch as a substantial amount of furniture was made in Lancaster for consignment to London by sea.

81. A, B. Sketch and estimate for 'A press bed in form of a desk' supplied by Gillow's in 1789; the bed made of deal (with some beech), and painted.

The Gillow Records (Estimate and Sketch Books).

Waring & Gillow, Ltd., Lancaster.

82. Lady's fall front secretary, of upright and rectangular form. The fall, which is quartered and finely figured, centres in a circular Wedgwood plaque of blue and white jasper ware. The piece is veneered with a variety of exotic woods, including 'flame' mahogany, rosewood, satinwood and amboyna; tulipwood is used for cross-bandings (as in the table drawer), boxwood and ebony for stringing lines. The metal mounts are chased and gilt. The galleried top is of grey marble. The piece resembles in form a *secrétaire à abattant*, fashionable in France from about 1760 to the time of the Revolution, and later, and clearly was inspired by French models. Much Louis XVI furniture is distinguished by the use of Sèvres porcelain as a means of decoration, and by fitted *ormolu* mounts. In England, the comparable practice of inserting Wedgwood plaques in furniture was followed.

Height, 4 ft. 2 in.

c. 1795.

83. 'A Horse Dressing Glass and Writing Table', of mahogany, supported on lyre-shaped standards. The character of the inlaid decoration is unusual.

The piece corresponds closely with a design, dated 1793, illustrated by Sheraton in the *Appendix* to the *Drawing Book*, Plate XVII. The 'convenience for writing', explains Sheraton, 'rises by a little horse. The dressing-boxes are made with close covers, and a slider incloses the whole, so that when the whole is turned up nothing can come out of its place. The glass . . . fixes in centers, so as to move in any position, either back or forward. And observe, that when the dressing flap is turned up it locks into the top rail. . . . The under side of the flap being the front when turned up, it may be japanned and banded . . . and to form the strings, brass wire is let in, which has a pretty effect.' The table, as executed, has been modified in some details, both of construction and ornament; and the curved feet of the standards are concave, not convex.

Height, 4 ft.; width, 2 ft. 1½ in.

c. 1795.

84. Clothes press, of mahogany; the base, supported on a low plinth, containing two short and two long drawers, fitted with small brass knob handles. The piece is bow-fronted, and of admirable proportions. The design is plain; and the decorative appearance of the front results largely from the employment of figured veneers.

c. 1800.

85. Clothes press, of mahogany, elaborately inlaid with various woods; the base supported on 'French' bracket feet, united by an apron piece; the upper stage surmounted by a lunette-shaped pediment centring in a tablet, with urns at the corners, above a 'Gothic' cornice.

Bearing the label (printed by 'Darling & Robinson, Gt. Newport St., London') of 'Mant, Upholder & Cabinet Maker, High Street, Winchester'. John Mant, included in the list of Freemen of the City in 1791, and later Mayor for a number of terms, was also an appraiser, auctioneer and, possibly, a retailer of London made furniture.

The piece corresponds in some features with Shearer's design for 'A Wing Clothes Press', contained in *The Cabinet-Makers' London Book of Prices*, 2nd ed., 1793, Plate 3 (Plate 67).

c. 1795.

86. Night table, of satinwood, with pierced tray top; decorated with panels of mahogany, and boxwood and ebony stringing lines; supported on 'panelled' taper legs.

Height, 2 ft. 5 in.; width, 1 ft. 2 in.; depth, 1 ft. ½ in.

c. 1790.

87. One of a pair of bow-fronted commodes, of harewood and satinwood; made for Margaretta Henrietta, wife of Sir George Buchan-Hepburn, 1st Baronet, of Smeaton House, Midlothian. The commode corresponds quite closely with a design by Sheraton for a similar article of furniture, dated 1792, in the *Drawing Book*, Plate XLIII (upper right); in the latter, however, part of the superstructure is enclosed at the back by small doors and the lower cupboard fitted with sliding tambour front. Sheraton remarks that 'these [pieces] are used in genteel bed-rooms, and are sometimes finished in satin-wood, and in a style a little elevated above their use'. He continues: 'The two drawers below the cupboard are real. The partititions may be cross-banded, and a string

round the corners of the drawer. These feet are turned, but sometimes they are made square. Sometimes there are folding doors to the cupboard part, and sometimes a curtain of green silk, fixed on a brass wire at top and bottom; but in this design a tambour door is used, as preferable. The upper cupboard contains shelves, and is intended to keep medicines to be taken in the night, or to hold other little articles which servants are not permitted to overlook.'

Height, 4 ft.; width, 1 ft. 5 in.

c. 1795.

88. Corner washstand ('corner enclosed bason-stand'), painted or japanned in various colours on a buff ground.

The front is convex, with a door in the centre. The lid, which encloses an interior fitted with spaces for a basin and two small dishes, is composed of two hinged portions, which lift up to form a back.

Height, 2 ft. 7½ in.

c. 1790.

Victoria and Albert Museum.

89. Engraved design for 'A Lady's Dressing Table', undated, by Thomas Sheraton, from the *Drawing Book*, Plate XLVI.

'These tables', states Sheraton, 'are often made of satin-wood, and banded; but sometimes . . . of mahogany. The size . . . which is here three feet, should be increased in its length near six inches when these folding side-glasses are introduced. The reason of this is, that a lady may have more room to sit between them to dress. It should, in this case, be made about two inches wider. But, observe, the size here given is that which is used when only the rising back-glass is introduced; and this has been the common way of finishing them. These side-glasses are an addition of my own, which I take to be an improvement; judging that, when they are finished in this manner, they will answer the end of a Rudd's table, at a less expence.'

Details of the construction are shown in the plan attached. The looking glass at the back 'rises up like that of a shaving-stand'; those at the sides, which are hinged to sliding stretchers, fold down and are stowed in positions 'A' and 'B'. The top is in three parts and, when closed, is locked at the centre, the sides being then secured by projecting tenons — 'as may be seen at the edge of the left-hand one'. The kneehole cupboard, which is reeded 'in the hollow part to imitate tambour', says Sheraton, 'will take a lady's hat as they wear them now.'

Sheraton's corrections, made in the text, are of some interest. The design was faulty, and the measurements of the piece, as indicated on the plate, required to be amended — 'observe, the size here given is that which is used when only the rising back-glass is introduced'. Presumably, he was not in a position to withdraw the plate.

90. A, B. (A) Engraved design for three 'Corner Bason-Stands', dated 1792, by Thomas Sheraton, from the *Drawing Book*, Plate XLII.

(B) Engraved designs for 'A Serpentine Dressing Chest, with straight Wings' and 'A Serpentine Dressing Chest, with ogee Ends', dated 1788, by Thomas Shearer, from *The Cabinet-Makers' London Book of Prices*, 2nd ed., 1793, Plate 20, Figs. 1 and 2. The latter piece contains a shelved cupboard in each end.

91. Engraved design for two dressing chests, dated 1793, by Thomas Sheraton, from the *Appendix* to the *Drawing Book*, Plate XV.

92. A, B. Sketch and estimate for 'A Japan'd satin wood Canterbury' supplied by Gillow's in 1793.

The piece is costed at £1 8s.; the wood required (mahogany, satinwood and oak boards, of various thicknesses) is valued at little more than 6s.; and the brass work is comparatively expensive. Later annotations on the record refer to a plain mahogany Canterbury ordered in 1804.

The Gillow Records (Estimate and Sketch Books).

Waring & Gillow, Ltd., Lancaster.

The term 'Canterbury', notes Sheraton in the *Cabinet Dictionary*, 'has of late years been applied to some pieces of cabinet work, because, as the story goes, the bishop of that see first gave orders for these pieces. One piece is a small music stand, with two or three hollow topped partitions, framed in light slips of mahogany, about three inches apart from each other, and about 8 inches deep, for holding music books. These have sometimes a small drawer, 3 inches deep, and the whole length of it, which is 18 inches; its width 12 inches, and the whole height 20 inches. The legs are made of $1\frac{1}{8}$ mahogany, turned or plain, tapered, with castors, and are adapted to run in under a piano-forte. The other piece . . . is a supper tray. . . .'

93. A, B. Sketch and estimate for 'A Pear Tree trunk' supplied by Gillow's to 'Dan¹. Wilson Esqʳᵉ.' in 1789.

The 'trunk' is an unusual small piece, made apparently to special order, and having much the same form and dimensions as some small tripod tables.

The curved 'claws' are of pear wood; the trunk itself is constructed of mahogany, veneered with pear wood.

Pear wood is close-grained, similar to boxwood, but is softer and, in colour, darker and tinged with red; it has little figure but was used occasionally as a veneer, mainly in the seventeenth century for long-case clocks, and in the country.

The Gillow Records (Estimate and Sketch Books).

Waring & Gillow, Ltd., Lancaster.

94. A, B. Wall mirror, the frame gilt and painted, within the mouldings, with an oviform design of grapes, flowers and terminals in colour on a pale yellow ground. Incorporated in the design at top and sides are three ovals of classical subjects; these are stipple engravings, coloured. The base moulding is very narrow.

Height, 6 ft. 10½ in.; width, 3 ft. 7 in.

Late eighteenth century.

Lady Lever Art Gallery.

95. Wall mirror, with circular frame of carved and gilt pinewood, and convex glass.

The cavetto of the frame is carved with *paterae* and bordered on the inner side by a thin beading and, next to the glass, a reeded ebonized slip; the outer band is reeded and crossed by ribbons. The cresting consists of an eagle displayed, surmounting a vase, which springs from spreading acanthus foliage; it and the base are prominent features of the design. The mirror is of unusually large size.

Height, 8 ft. 4 in.

c. 1800.

Victoria and Albert Museum.

96. A, B. (A) Engraved design for 'A Dining Parlour in imitation of the Prince of Wales's', dated 1793, by Thomas Sheraton, from the *Drawing Book*, Plate LX.

'This method of representing a dining or drawing-room has its advantages . . . the end wall nearest the eye is supposed to be laid level with the floor, without which the inside of the room could not be seen . . . the walls, furniture, and every particular, are shewn in their natural position, except the first end, so that the effect of the whole may be better judged of than in the other method. . . . The Prince's has five windows facing St. James's Park. This also has five, one of which is hid by the left column. His windows are made to come down to the floor, which open in two parts as a double door, leading to a large grass plat to walk in. If I remember right', says Sheraton, 'there are pilasters between each window; but this is intended to have glass. In his is a large glass over the chimney-piece, as this has. To these glass frames are fixed candle-branches. At each end of his is a large sideboard, nearly twelve feet in length, standing between a couple of Ionic columns, worked in composition to imitate fine variegated marble, which have a most beautiful and magnificent effect.'

(B) Thomas Sheraton's Trade Card.

Size of original, $2\frac{1}{4} \times 3\frac{1}{8}$ in.

c. 1795–1800.

British Museum (formerly, Sir Ambrose Heal Collection).

SHORT BIBLIOGRAPHY

A. Hepplewhite and Co., *The Cabinet-Maker and Upholsterer's Guide; or Repository of Designs for Every Article of Household Furniture*, 1788; 2nd edition, 1789; 3rd edition, 1794.

Facsimile reprint of 3rd edition, Batsford, 1897.

Abridged edition, *Hepplewhite Furniture Designs*, with introduction by Ralph Edwards, Tiranti, 1947.

The Cabinet-Makers' London Book of Prices, 1788; 2nd edition, 1793.

Thomas Sheraton, *The Cabinet-Maker and Upholsterer's Drawing-Book*, with the *Appendix* and *An Accompaniment*, 1791–4; 2nd edition, 1794; 3rd edition, 1802.

Facsimile reprint of 3rd edition, Batsford, 1895.

Abridged edition, *Sheraton Furniture Designs*, with introduction by Ralph Edwards, Tiranti, 1945.

Thomas Sheraton, *The Cabinet Dictionary*, 1803.

Percy Macquoid and Ralph Edwards, *The Dictionary of English Furniture*, 3 vols., Country Life, 1924–7; revised edition by Ralph Edwards, 1954.

Percy Macquoid, *English Furniture, Tapestry and Needlework of the XVIth–XIXth Centuries. A Record of the Collection in the Lady Lever Art Gallery, Port Sunlight, formed by the First Viscount Leverhulme*, Batsford, 1928.

Ralph Edwards, *Victoria and Albert Museum: Catalogue of English Furniture and Woodwork*, Vol. IV, Georgian, H.M. Stationery Office, 1931.

H. Clifford Smith, *Buckingham Palace*, Country Life, 1931.

Ralph Edwards and Margaret Jourdain, *Georgian Cabinet-Makers*, Country Life, 1946; revised edition, 1955.

Sir Ambrose Heal, *The London Furniture Makers, 1660–1840*, Batsford, 1953.

Ralph Fastnedge, *English Furniture Styles*, Penguin Books, 1955; reprinted, 1961.

Peter Ward-Jackson, *English Furniture Designs of the Eighteenth Century*, H.M. Stationery Office, 1958.

INDEX

Note: *In subsidiary references, S. stands for Sheraton, and H. for Hepplewhite.*

Kenwood (Lord Mansfield), France & Beckwith furniture at, 37
Kevan, E. F., *London's Oldest Baptist Church*, 21, 21 n
Kidney tables, 29, 60, 97, Pls. 44, 45
Kingwood ('Kingswood'), 40, 44, 64, 94, 107
Knee-hole dressing chest, 74
Knee-hole (kidney) writing table, 18, Pl. 45
Knee-hole pedestal library tables, 64
Knife cases (S.), 27, 62 n; vases of sideboards serving as, 61

Labels identifying furniture, 15, 36
Laburnum wood, 44
Lady's (or ladies'): cabinets, 29, 105, 106, 107, Pls. 57B, 70, 71; writing cabinets, Pls. 72, 73; cabinet on stand, 102–3; dressing-tables, 111–112, Pl. 89; secretary, 109; writing-tables, work tables, 65, 66, 67, 99, 102, 103, 104, Pls. 56, 61, 64
Lancaster: Gillows of, 34, 35; *see* Gillow
Lane, John, 27
'Lazy tongs' principle (table extension), 59
Leaf, single pull-out ('Universal' table), 60
Legs (feet), characteristic (*see also* Feet): breakfast-table, 60–1; card-table, 55, 56; Casement's profiles, 18, Pl. 48 (*see* Thermed); of chairs generally, 50–2; claw, curved claw, 49, 100; curved square section, 87; cylindrical turned, 86; dining-table (of later period), 58–9; dressing-table, 74, 75; 'engaged' (sideboard), 63; ladies' writing-table, 67; library-table, 64, 65; Marlbro', 47, 48, 57, 96, 101; panelled taper, 102, 105, 110; Pembroke-table, 56; pier-table, 54, 55, 56; pillar and claw, 58, 59, 60, 94, 95; press-bed, 72; reeded, 100; sabre-shaped, 97; sideboard, 63; spindle, 88; tapered (plain), 86, 97, 101; tapered, bevelled at sides, 96; tapered, with castors, 112; tapered, panelled, 102, 105, 110; tapered, with spade feet, 89; tapered, of square section, 87, 103, 107; thermed, 98–9; three patterns for, 90. *See* Plates generally, especially 24, 48, 49
Leverhulme, the 1st Viscount, 27 n
Library cases, 68–70; Shearer's, 17
Library steps, 79, 94; Campbell's and Sheraton's 39; Hervé's, Pl. 3A, *and see* Hervé, Francis
Library tables, 64–5, 95; circular, 98; oval, 27; *see* Pls. 39, 47
Lion masks (S.), 83; with rings, 97, 99

Lion-paw foot, 83
Lobby chests, 73–4
London Cabinet-Makers' Union Book of Prices (1811, 1824, 1836, 1866), 85, Pls. 2, 40A
London Guide, 20 n
London Society of Cabinet-Makers, 16
London Tradesman, The (1747), 13
Long-case clocks, 78–9, 104, Pl. 65
'Long-way' mouldings, 48
Loo table, 95, 98
Louis XVI furniture, 28, 89, 109, Pl. 21
Lyre-shaped supports, ends, 29, 57, 99, 109

Macquoid, Percy, *The Age of Satinwood*, 107; *English Furniture, Tapestry and Needlework of the XVIth–XIXth Centuries*, 115; (with Ralph Edwards): *The Dictionary of English Furniture*, 115
Mahogany, 40–2; prices, 44; for pier tables, 54; for clock cases, 78. *See* Pls. 6, 7, 10, 11, 13, 22, 23, 36, 37, 40, 46, 52, 53, 68, 76, 78, 83, 84, 85
Manilla wood, *see* Satinwood
Maple: veneer, *see* Harewood, 43; *see also* Oxide of copper
Marble-topped pier tables, 54
Maria Louisa, Queen of Spain, 27
'Marlbro'' leg, 47, 48, 57, 96, 101
Marquetry, 41, 45, 46, 95
Marsh, *see* Elward Marsh & Co.
Marshall, William, 37; *On Planting and Rural Ornament*, 40
Mayhew, John, 38, 39, 40
McLean & Son, John, 36
Memoirs of Adam Black, 22–3
'Mendlesham' chairs, 80, 81, 88, Pl. 14
Mirrors, 76–7, 85, 113, Pls. 3, 94, 95
Moore, William (Dublin cabinet-maker), 55 n
Morel, Nicholas, 39
Motifs (H. and S.), 28–9
Moulding, 48; moulding planes, 48
'Moving libraries', 70
Musical box, in cabinet, 107
Music stands, 100, 101, Pl. 56

Needlework-covered mahogany stool, 90, Pl. 22
Nelson, Lord, funeral furnishing for, 37
Nelson, S., 39
Neo-classicism of 1780's, 16, 18
Nicholson, Alexander (editor and writer of Adam Black's *Memoirs*), 23

INDEX

PLATES

1. 'The Cabinet-maker'. Engraving; dated 1804.

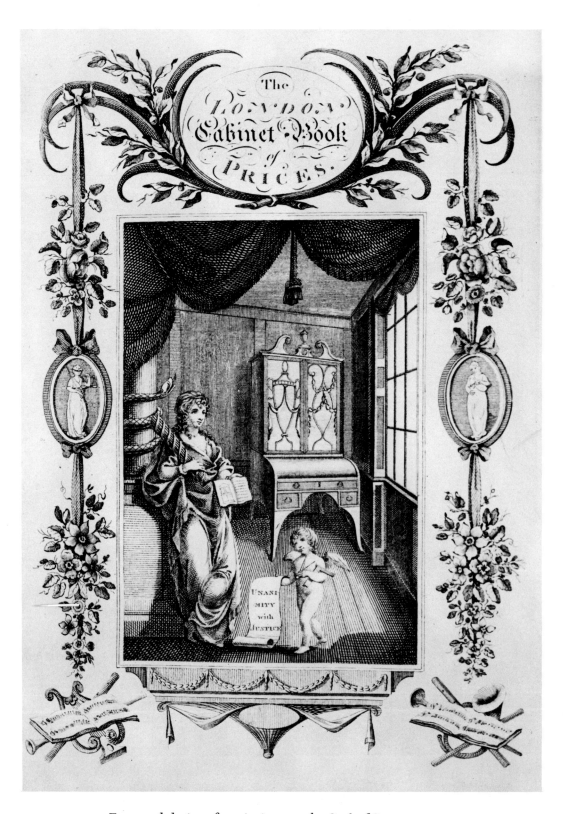

2. Engraved design, frontispiece to the *Book of Prices*; *c.* 1788.

3. Design for a mirror; *c.* 1790, Inscribed: 'Thos. Sheraton'.
Victoria and Albert Museum.

4. Stockton High Street. Engraving, after 'T. Sheraton'; *c. 1785.*
Public Libraries, Museum and Art Gallery, Stockton-on-Tees.

5. 'The Breakfast Room' at Pitzhanger Manor, Ealing; 1802.
Sir John Soane's Museum.

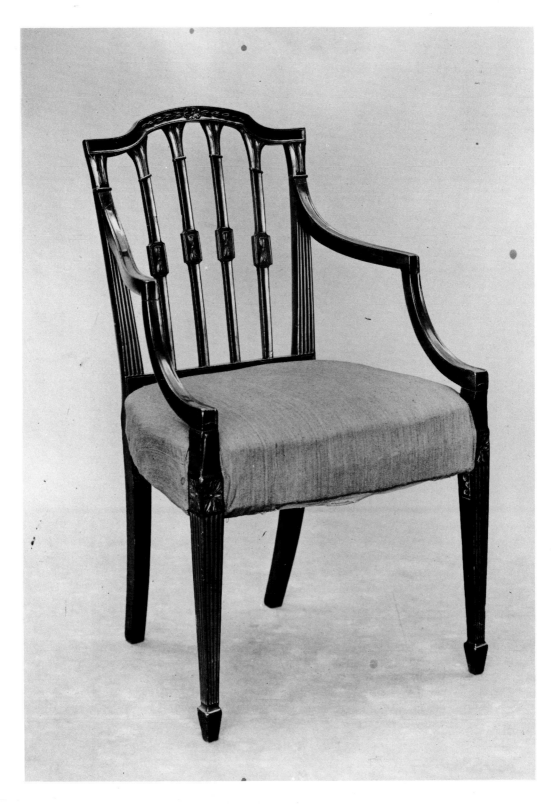

6. Mahogany armchair; *c.* 1790–5.
Victoria and Albert Museum.

7. Mahogany chair. Inscribed: 'Samuel Fairhead August 1783'.
Victoria and Albert Museum.

8. Painted satinwood chair, based on a *Drawing Book* design; *c. 1795.*
Metropolitan Museum of Art, New York (Fletcher Fund, 1929).

9. Armchair of beech wood, japanned and gilt; *c.* 1800.
Victoria and Albert Museum.

10. Mahogany chair, based on a Hepplewhite design dated *1787*.
Victoria and Albert Museum.

11. Mahogany hall chair; *c.* 1800.
Victoria and Albert Museum.

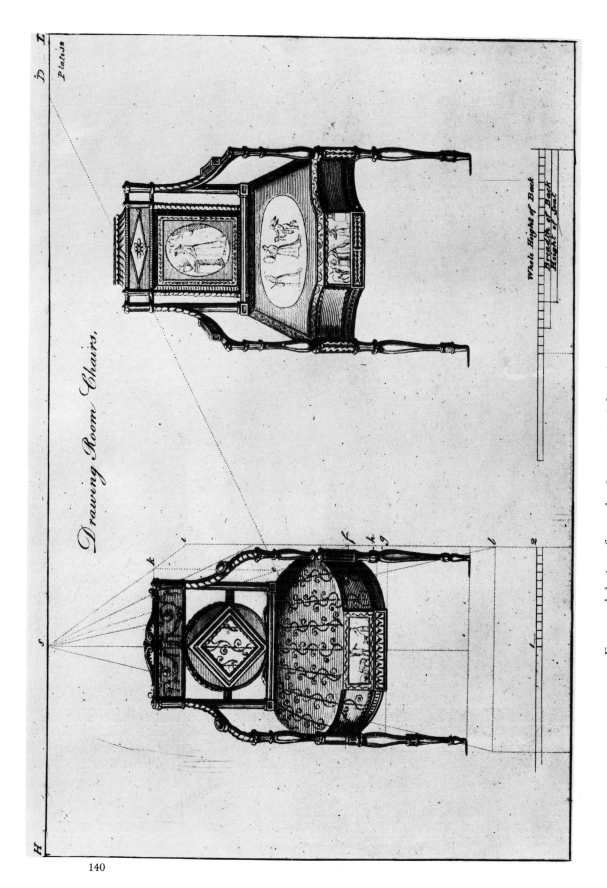

12. Engraved designs from the *Drawing Book* for a 'Drawing Room Chair';
dated 1792.

13. Mahogany trellis back chair, by John Robins; 1828.
Armchair of similar pattern; c. 1810.
Sir John Soane's Museum.

14. 'Mendlesham' armchair, of yew, with elm seat; *c.* 1800.
Ayer & Co. Ltd., Bath.

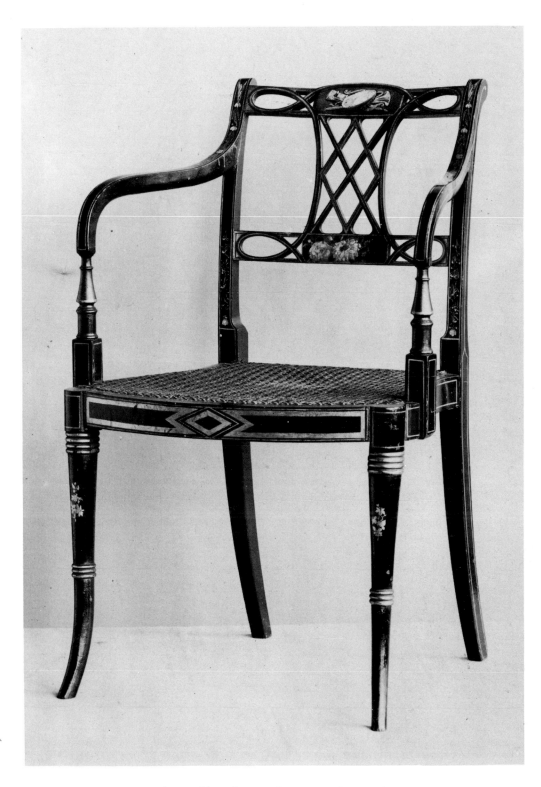

15. Armchair of beech wood, japanned and gilt; *c.* 1800.
Victoria and Albert Museum.

16. Armchair of cast iron; early nineteenth century.
Sir John Soane's Museum.

17. Chair of imitation bamboo, supplied by Elward, Marsh and Tatham
for Brighton Pavilion in 1802.
Royal Pavilion Committee, Brighton Corporation

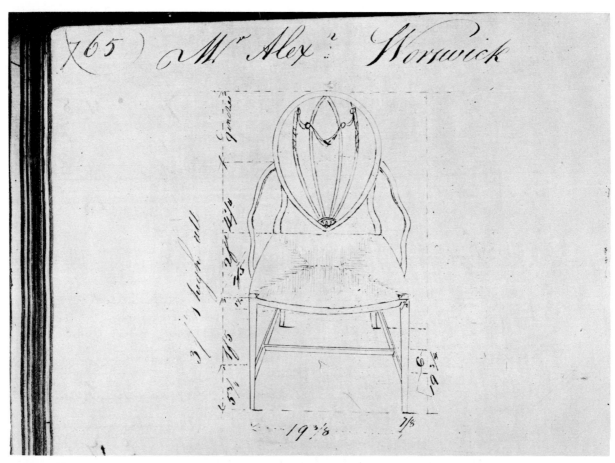

18. Sketch and estimate for 'A Painted chair' made by Gillow's in 1791.
Waring & Gillow, Ltd., Lancaster.

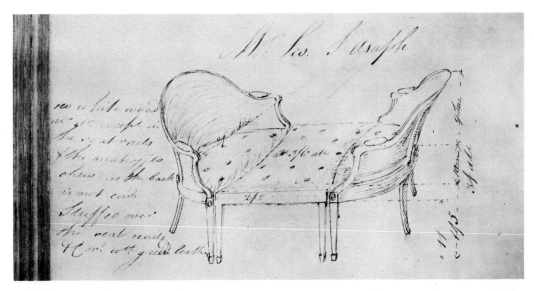

19. Sketch and estimate for a *duchesse* made by Gillow's in 1793.
Waring & Gillow, Ltd., Lancaster.

20. Settee of japanned beech wood; c. 1790–5.
Victoria and Albert Museum.

148

21. Sofa, upholstered with Beauvais tapestry, by Georges Jacob;
French, period of Louis XVI.
Reproduced by permission of the Trustees of the Wallace Collection.

22. Mahogany stool, covered with needlework; *c.* 1800.
Lady Lever Art Gallery.

23. Mahogany stool of 'X' form; *c.* 1805.
Lady Lever Art Gallery.

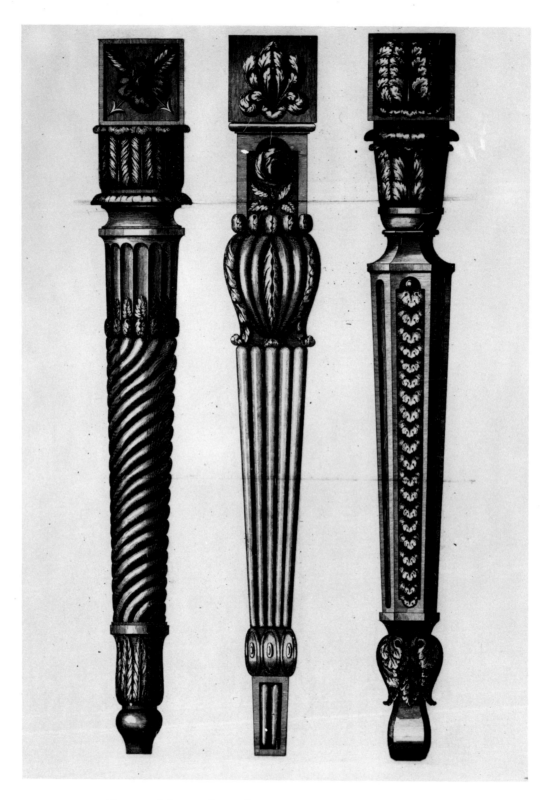

24. Engraved design from the *Accompaniment* to the *Drawing Book* for 3 patterns for chair legs; dated 1793.

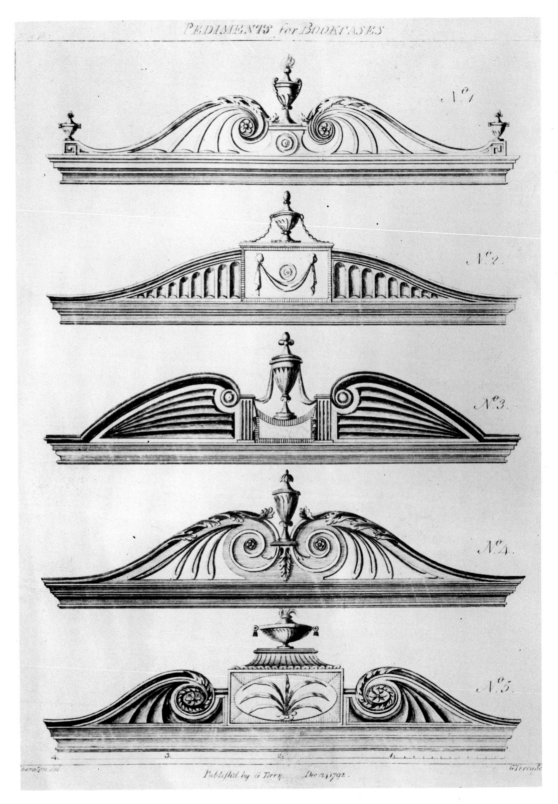

Published by G. Terry. Dec. 24, 1792.

25. Engraved design from the *Drawing Book* for 5 patterns for
'Pediments for Bookcases'; dated 1792.

26. Part of an engraved design from the *Drawing Book* for
'A Plan & Section of a Drawing Room' of a town house; dated 1793.

27. Engraved design from the *Appendix* to the *Drawing Book*:
'A View of the South End of the Prince of Wales's Chinese Drawing Room'
in Carlton House; dated 1793.

28A. Painted side table, of birch coloured to resemble satinwood;
c. 1790–1800.
28B. Detail of the top.
Lady Lever Art Gallery.

156

29A. Carved and gilt side table, with painted decoration, supplied
for Carlton House, probably to the design of Henry Holland; *c.* 1795.
29B. Detail of the top.
Metropolitan Museum of Art, New York (Fletcher Fund, 1929).

30. Commode, painted with figure subjects after Angelica Kauffmann
on a pea-green ground; c. 1790.
Lady Lever Art Gallery.

31. Satinwood dwarf bookcase; *c.* 1790.
At Buckingham Palace.
Reproduced by gracious permission of H.M. The Queen.

32A. Lady's dressing commode of painted satinwood; *c.* 1790.

32B. Detail of the top.

Lady Lever Art Gallery.

33A. Top of commode, with inlaid decoration of coloured woods
in a ground of harewood; *c.* 1780.
Lady Lever Art Gallery.

33B. Top of satinwood side table; *c.* 1790.
Ayer & Co. Ltd., Bath.

33C. Top of commode of modified serpentine form; *c.* 1790.
Jeremy, Ltd., London, S.W.3.

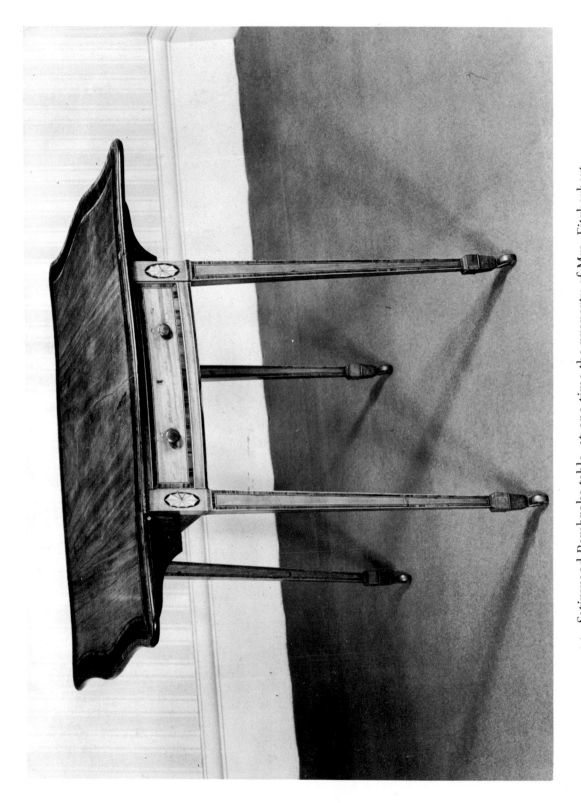

34. Satinwood Pembroke table, at one time the property of Mrs. Fitzherbert, at Brighton; c. 1790.

Royal Pavilion Committee, Brighton Corporation.

162

35. Satinwood tea table; c. 1795–1800.
At Buckingham Palace.
Reproduced by gracious permission of H.M. The Queen.

36A. Mahogany library steps, by Francis Hervé; *c.* 1790.
36B. The steps closed.
Victoria and Albert Museum.

37. Mahogany breakfast table; *c. 1795–1800.*
Details of three 'pillar-and-claw' supports, of comparable date.
M. Harris & Sons, London, W.C.1.

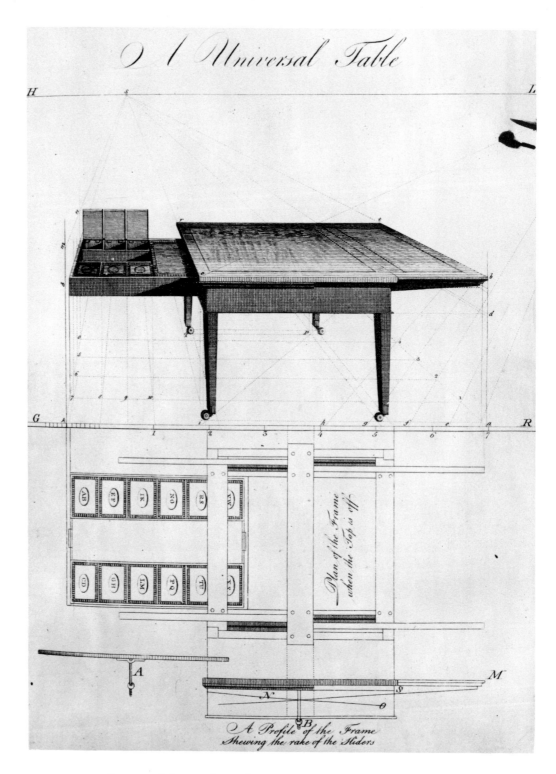

38. Engraved design from the *Drawing Book* for 'A Universal Table';
dated 1791.

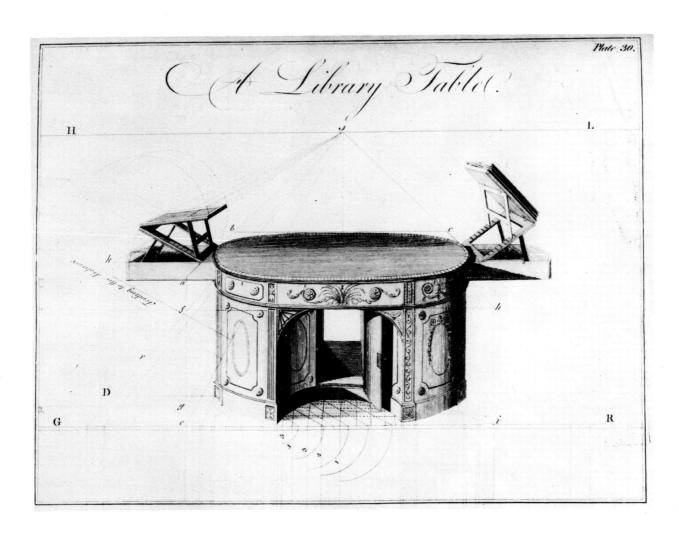

39. Engraved design from the *Drawing Book* for 'A Library Table';
dated 1791.

40A. Mahogany cellaret sideboard, based on a design in the *Book of Prices*,
dated 1788.
Lady Lever Art Gallery.
40B. Mahogany cellaret sideboard; *c.* 1795.

Victoria and Albert Museum.

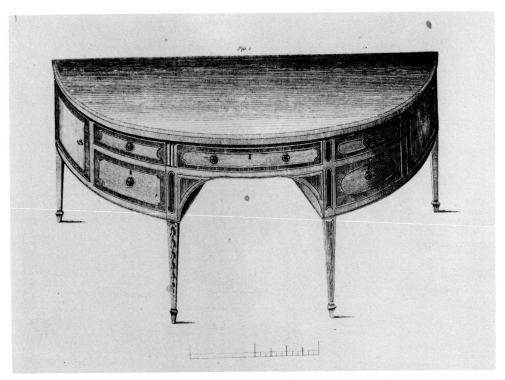

41. Engraved designs for a cellaret sideboard, by Shearer,
from the *Book of Prices*; dated 1788.

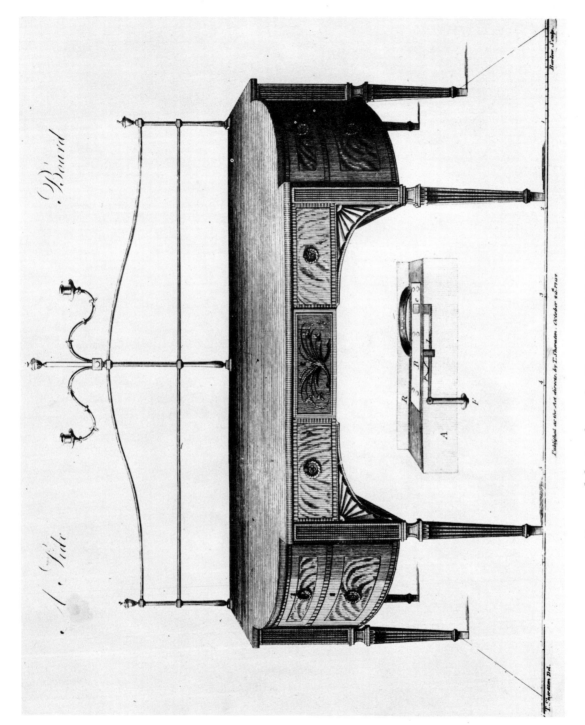

42. Engraved design from the *Drawing Book* for 'A Side Board';
dated 1792.

43. Engraved design from the *Cabinet Dictionary* for a 'Grecian Dining Table'; dated 1803.

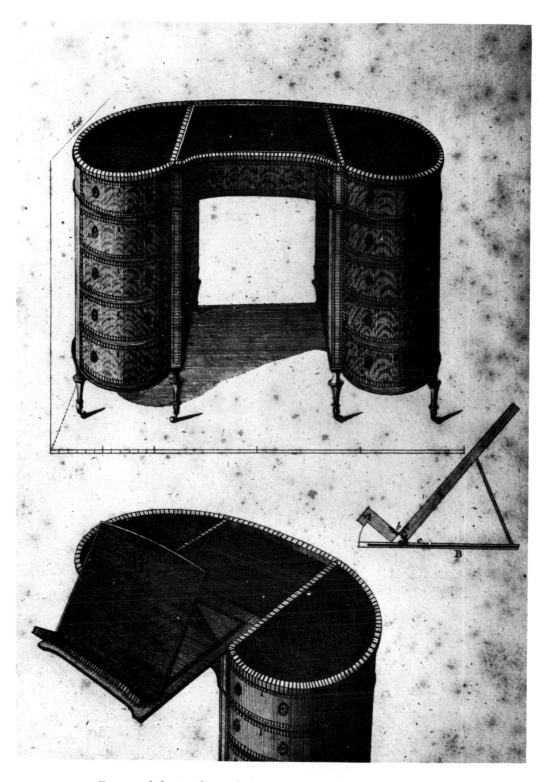

44. Engraved design from the *Drawing Book* for 'A Kidney Table';
dated 1792.

45. Engraved designs for 'A Gentleman's Social Table' and
'A Knee-Hole Kidney Library Writing Table', by 'Heppelwhite',
from the *Book of Prices*; dated 1792.

46. 'Carlton House' mahogany writing table, based on a design in the *Book of Prices*, dated 1792. *Phillips of Hitchin, Ltd.*

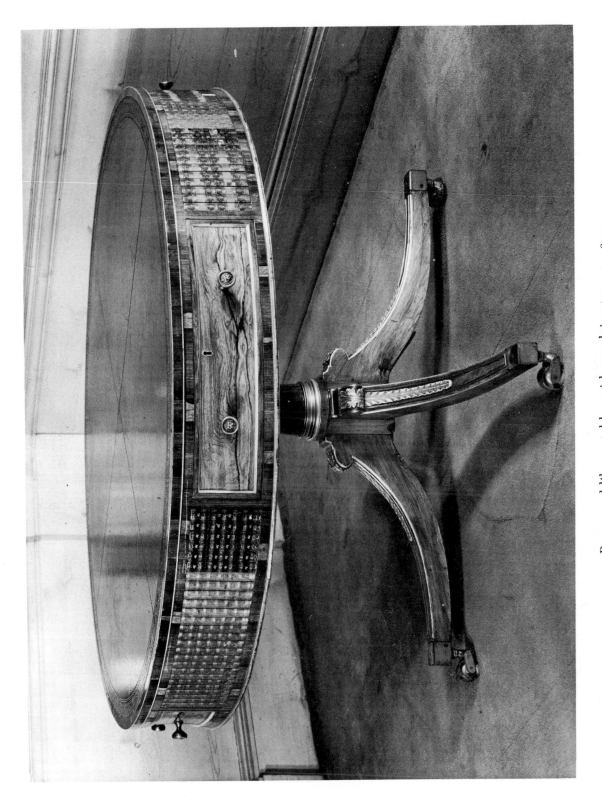

47. Rosewood library table, with revolving top; c. 1800.
At Buckingham Palace.
Reproduced by gracious permission of H.M. The Queen.

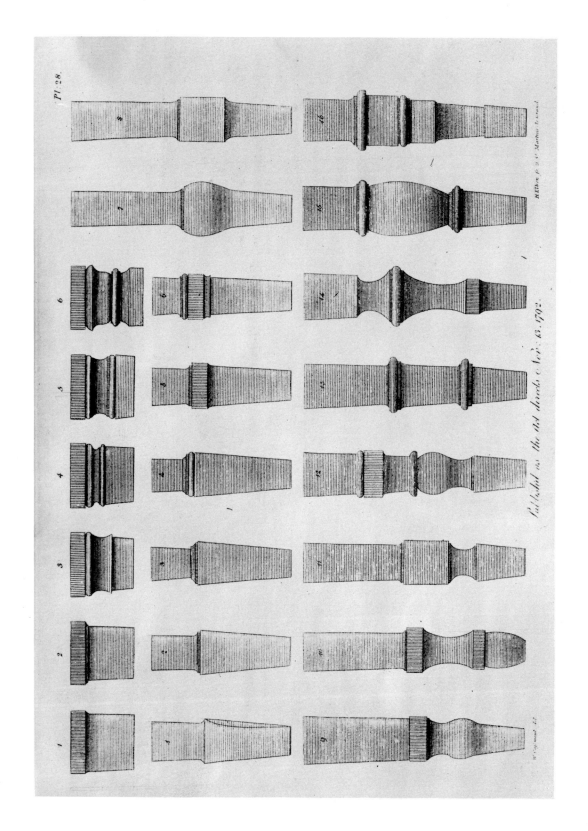

48. Engraved design for 16 patterns for 'thermed' legs, by Casement, from the *Book of Prices*; dated 1792.

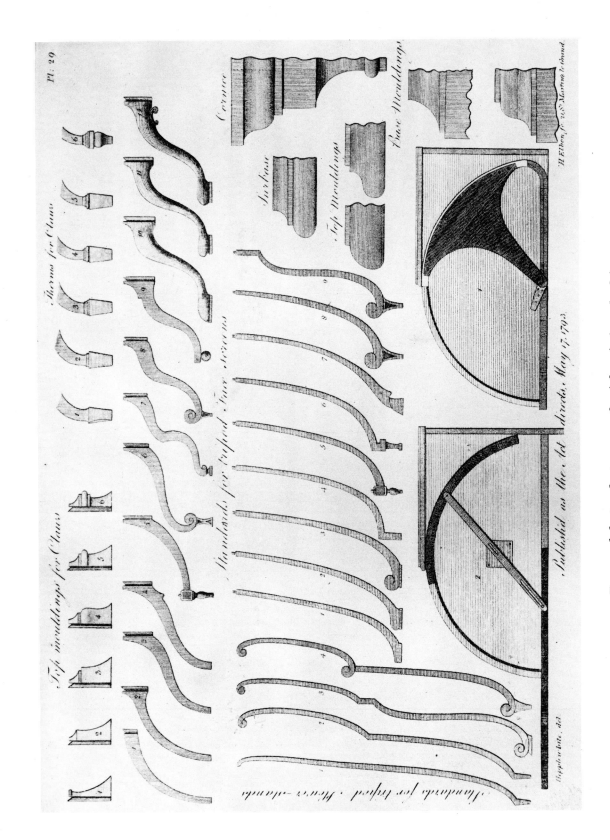

49. Engraved design for patterns for 'claws', 'standards', etc., by 'Hepplewhite', from the *Book of Prices*; dated 1793.

50. Lady's work table, of satinwood; *c*. 1790.
Victoria and Albert Museum.

51. Satinwood work table, of the '*tricoteuse*' type; *c. 1795.*
Ayer & Co. Ltd., Bath.

52. Mahogany work table; *c.* 1805–10.
Lady Lever Art Gallery.

53. Terrestrial globe, supported on mahogany stand; *c.* 1800.
Victoria and Albert Museum.

54. Set of satinwood 'quartetto' tables,
corresponding with a *Cabinet Dictionary* design; *c.* 1805.
The Connoisseur.

55. Rosewood drum-top table; *c.* 1800.
Royal Pavilion Committee, Brighton Corporation.

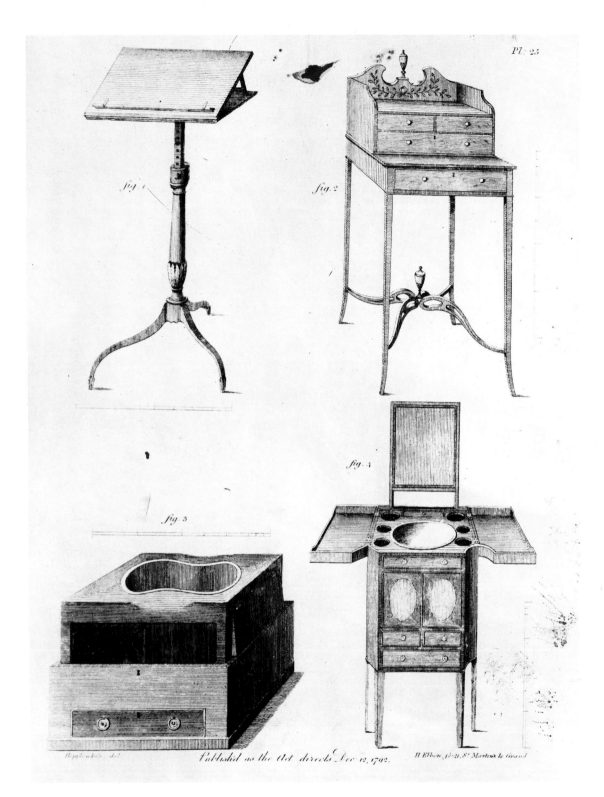

56. Engraved designs for 'A Music Stand', 'A Lady's Work Table', 'A Travelling Bidet' and 'A Shaving Stand', by 'Hepplewhite', from the *Book of Prices*; dated 1792.

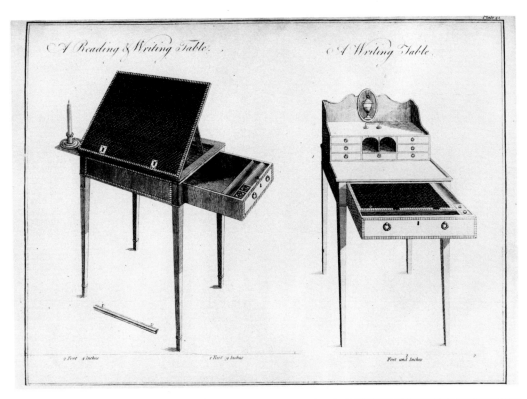

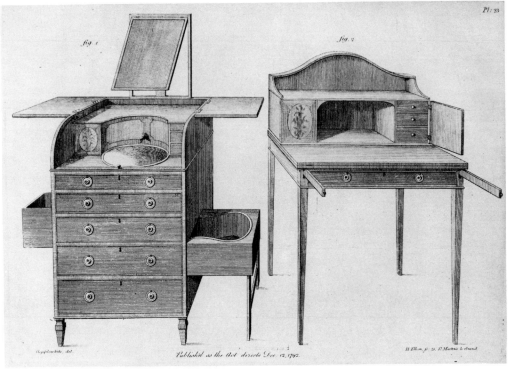

57A. Engraved designs from the *Drawing Book* for
'A Reading & Writing Table' and 'A Writing Table'; dated 1792.
57B. Engraved designs for a cylinder-fall wash-hand dressing chest and
'A Lady's Cabinet', by 'Hepplewhite', from the *Book of Prices*; dated 1792.

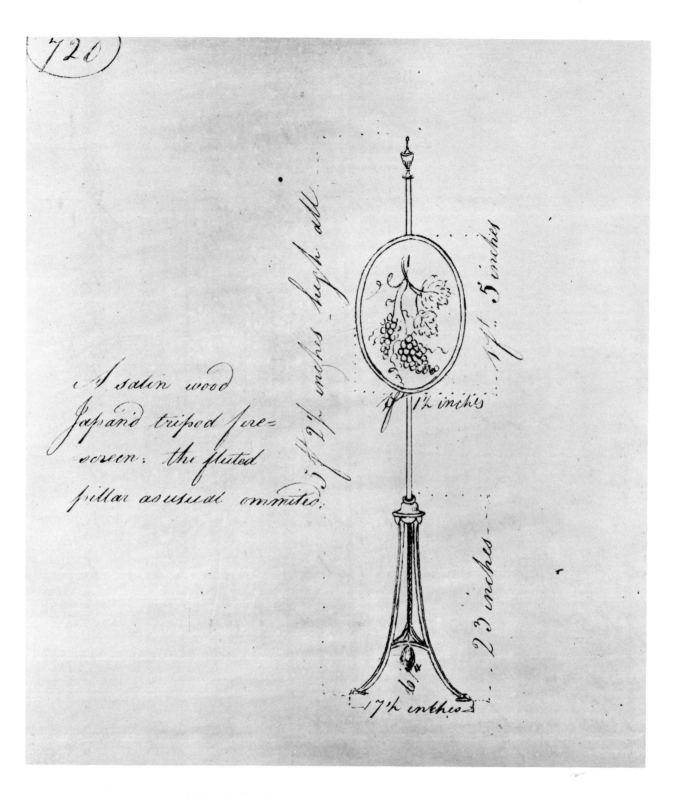

58. Sketch for 'A satin wood Japan'd tripod fire screen'
made by Gillow's in 1791.
Waring & Gillow, Ltd., Lancaster.

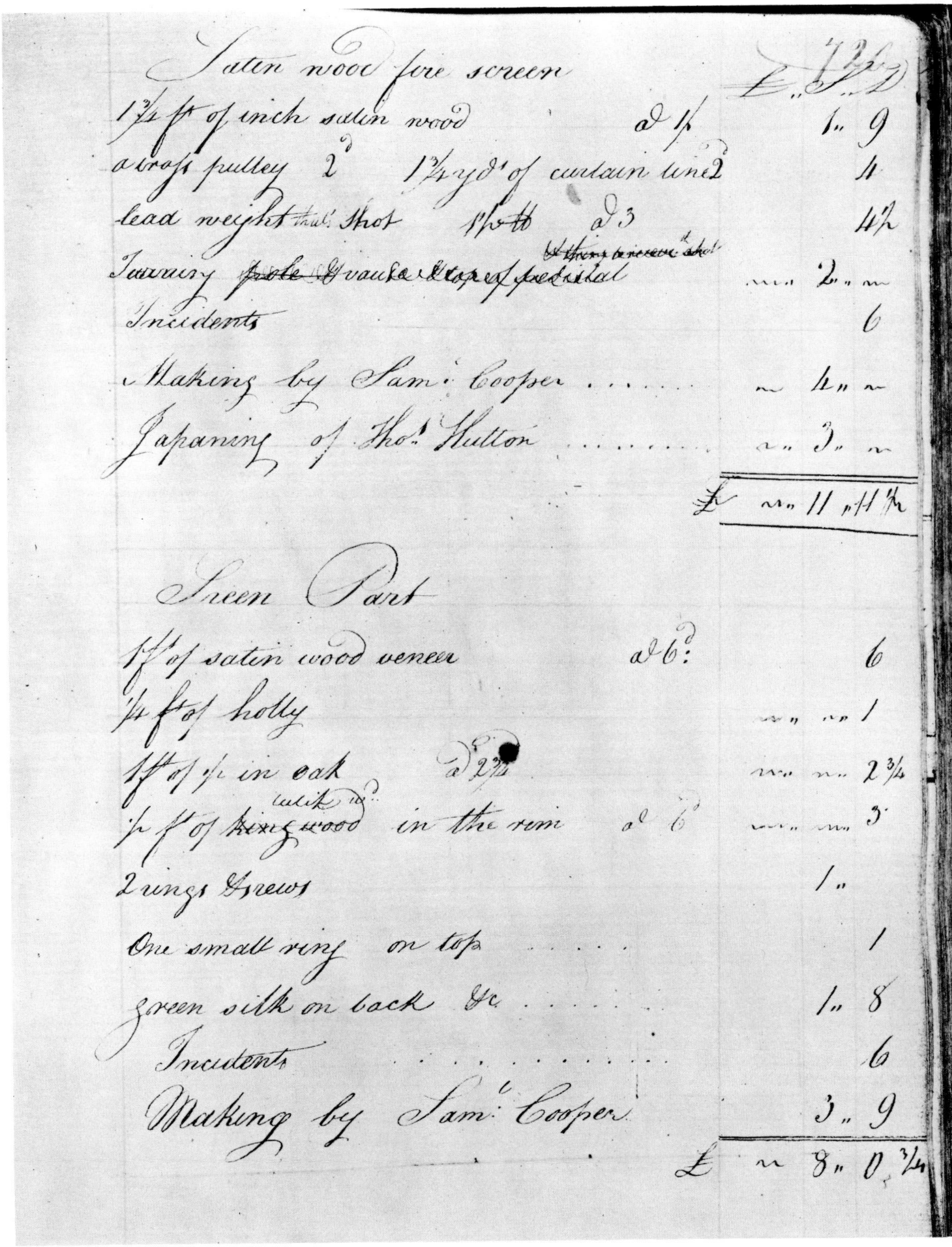

Saten wood fire screen	£	s	d
1¾ ft of inch satin wood at 1/		1	9
a cross pulley 2d 1¼ yds of curtain line			4
lead weight ~~that~~ Shot 1½ lb at 3			4½
Turning ~~pole~~ & vause & top of pedestal		2	
Incidents			6
Making by Saml Cooper		4	
Japaning of Thos Hutton		3	
£		11	11½

Sreen Part	£	s	d
1 ft of satin wood veneer at 6d			6
¼ ft of holly			1
1 ft of ½ in oak at 2¾			2¾
½ ft of ~~kingwood~~ in the rim at 6			3
2 rings & screws		1	
One small ring on top			1
green silk on back &c		1	8
Incidents			6
Making by Saml Cooper		3	9
£		8	0¾

59. Estimate for Pl. 58.

60. Lady's cylinder desk, veneered with rosewood and satinwood; *c.* 1800.
Norman Adams, Ltd., London, S.W.3.

61. Lady's satinwood writing table, by Gillow's; *c.* 1790–1800.
Norman Adams, Ltd., London, S.W.3.

62. Painted cabinet on stand, onetime the property of James Hook,
the composer; c. 1790.
Lady Lever Art Gallery.

63. Satinwood bookstand, with cupboard base; *c. 1795.*
The Connoisseur.

64. Lady's writing table, of rosewood, based on a *Drawing Book* design; *c.* 1805.
M. Harris & Sons, London, W.C.1.

65. Balloon long-case clock, with 'regulator' movement
by Thomas Iles, London; *c. 1795.*
Ayer & Co. Ltd., Bath.

66. Engraved designs for a bureau bookcase, by Shearer, from the *Book of Prices*; dated 1788.

194

67. Engraved design for a wardrobe, by Shearer, from the *Book of Prices*; dated 1788.

68. Mahogany bookcase; *c.* 1795.
Ayer & Co. Ltd., Bath.

69. Satinwood china cabinet; *c.* 1790.
Jeremy, Ltd., London, S.W.3.

A Cabinet.

From S to d is only half the whole distance.

70. Engraved design from the *Drawing Book* for a lady's cabinet; *c.* 1792.

71. Engraved design from the *Cabinet Dictionary* for a lady's cabinet;
dated 1802.

72. Lady's writing cabinet, veneered with satinwood
and elaborately inlaid with various woods; *c. 1795.*
Phillips of Hitchin, Ltd.

73. Lady's writing cabinet, veneered with satinwood,
with painted decoration; *c.* 1795.
Lady Lever Art Gallery.

74. Bureau cabinet, of yew; *c.* 1785.
Phillips of Hitchin, Ltd.

75. Cabinet, veneered with satinwood and sacquebu; *c. 1795.*
By permission of the Museum and Art Gallery, Birmingham.

76. Mahogany cylinder bookcase, based on a *Cabinet Dictionary* design; *c.* 1803.
Apollo.

77. Chamber organ, by James Hancock; dated 1788.
Royal Pavilion Committee, Brighton Corporation.

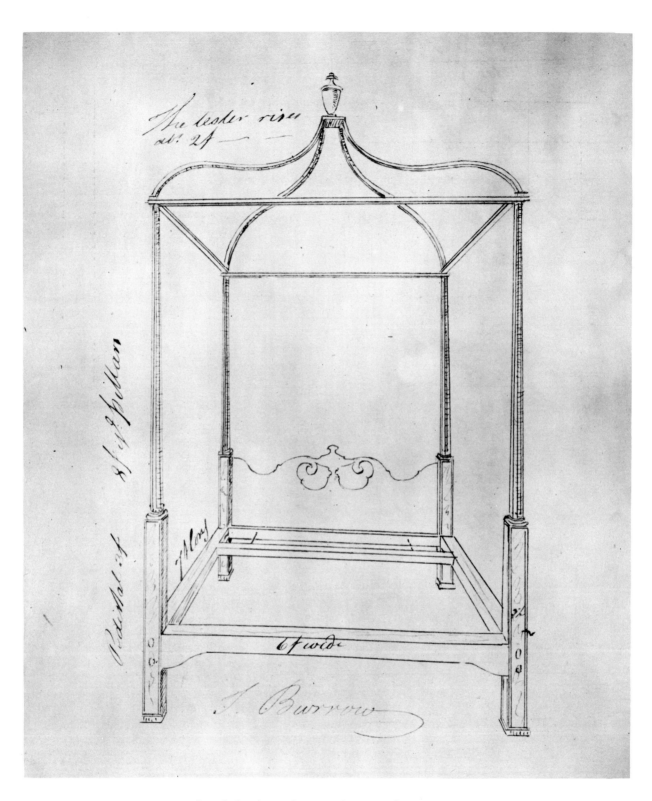

78. Sketch for 'A mahog. Bedstead wth reeded pillars'
made by Gillow's in 1793.
Waring & Gillow, Ltd., Lancaster.

Estimate of Bedstead with reeded pillars

35 ft of ½ inch dto hard wood mahogany Pillars 9d ... 1 . 8 . 6

29½ ft of inch dto hard wood sides &c a 9d ... 1 . 2 . 1½

4¾ ft of 2½ by 3½ inch mahogany Gluing ... . 2 . 10

19½ ft of inch mahogany & 1½ do in Tester 8d ... . 13 . —

1 ft of ¾ do head board a ½ ... . 11 . —

16 ft of venr wt bands a 5 ... . 6 . 8

106 ft of String of 3 thread at 1 ... . 8 . 10

2 Doz puties 2d .... 6 brass Conductors 3½=2d ... 3 . 9

16 bed screws 3 4d ..... 2 drawnail do 6d =13 ... . 5 . 1

16 brass screws even 1 16 .... 4 brass hoops do ... . 2 . —

One set of Iron casters 20d .... 4 Pikes 4 ... . 2 . —

Turning by Duke Ball ... . 5 . 6

Painting by J. Wilks   Compute ... de

Varnishing by Thos Romney ... . 2 . 6

Incidents ... . 2 . 6

Making by John Malley   compute ... de . de

                                                  £ 7 . 13 . 5½

Turning a small oar to stand upon do ... 9

Tester do wood in do 5 ...

                                                  £ 7 . 14 . 2½

Sail cloth bed bottom

79. Estimate for Pl. 78.

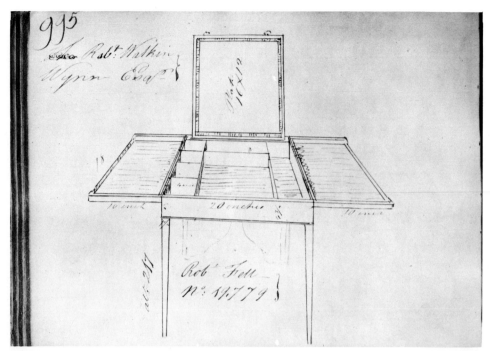

80. Sketch and estimate for 'A white wood Japan'd dressing table'
made by Gillow's in 1793.
Waring & Gillow, Ltd., Lancaster.

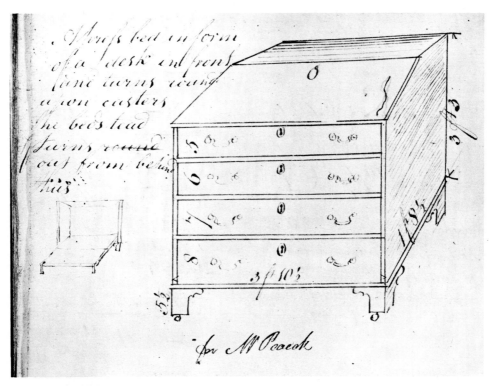

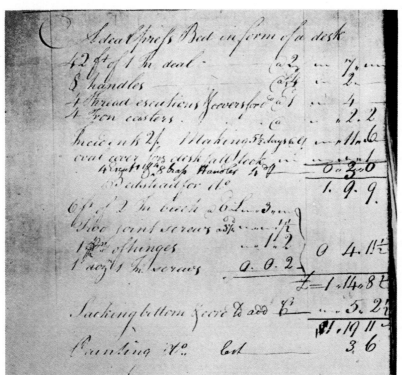

81. Sketch and estimate for a press bed made by Gillow's in 1789.
Waring & Gillow, Ltd., Lancaster.

82. Fall front secretary, of a type inspired by French models; *c. 1795.*
Jeremy, Ltd., London, S.W.3.

83. Mahogany cheval dressing table, based on a *Drawing Book* design; *c. 1795.*
Ayer & Co. Ltd., Bath.

84. Mahogany clothes press; *c. 1800.*
Phillips of Hitchin, Ltd.

85. Mahogany clothes press, inlaid with various woods; *c. 1795.*
Phillips of Hitchin, Ltd.

86. Satinwood night table; *c.* 1790.
The Connoisseur.

87. Commode, of harewood and satinwood, based on a *Drawing Book* design;

c. 1795.

H. C. Baxter & Sons, London, S.W.5.

88. Painted corner washstand; *c.* 1790.
Victoria and Albert Museum.

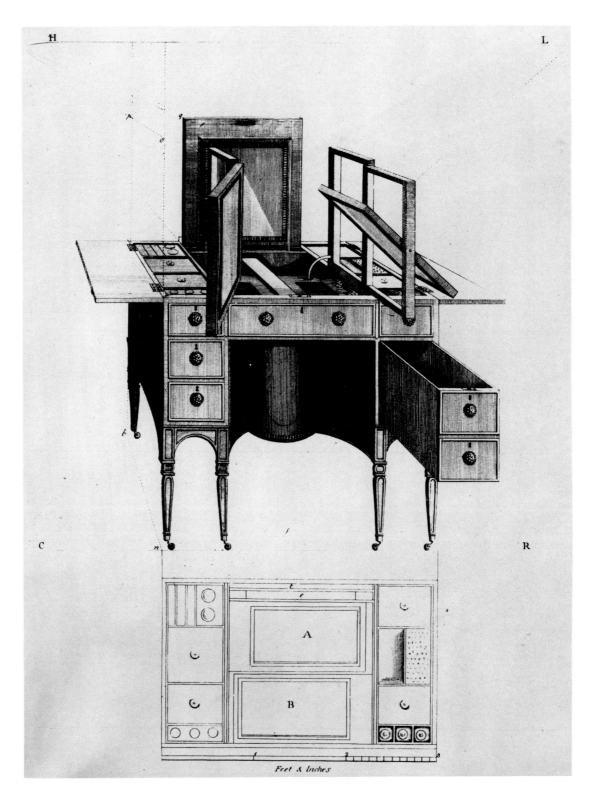

89. Engraved design from the *Drawing Book* for a lady's dressing table.

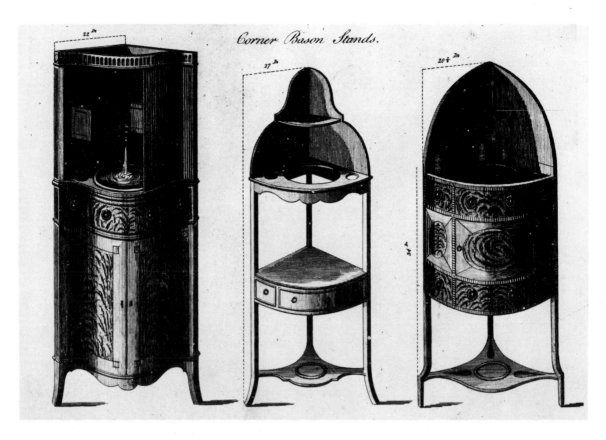

90A. Engraved designs from the *Drawing Book* for a 'Corner Bason-Stand';
dated 1792.

90B. Engraved designs for a dressing chest, by Shearer, from the *Book of Prices*;
dated 1788.

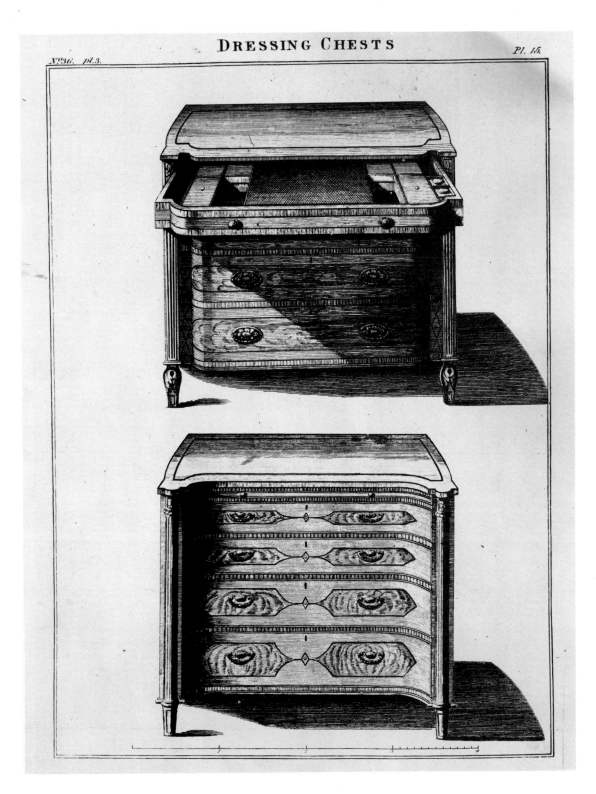

91. Engraved designs from the *Drawing Book* for a dressing chest; dated 1793.

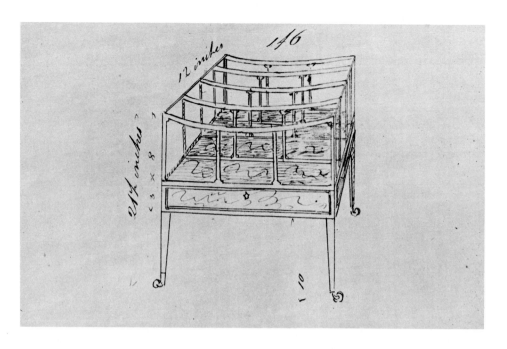

92. Sketch and estimate for 'A Japan'd satin wood Canterbury'
made by Gillow's in 1793.
Waring & Gillow, Ltd., Lancaster.

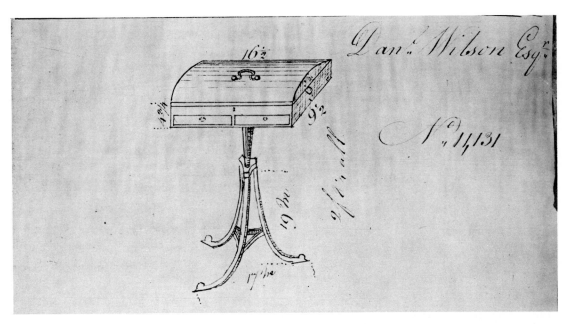

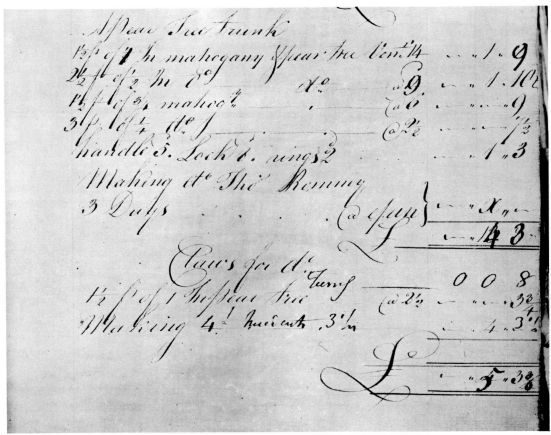

93. Sketch and estimate for 'A Pear Tree trunk' made by Gillow's in 1789.
Waring & Gillow, Ltd., Lancaster.

94A. Wall mirror, with painted decoration; late eighteenth century.
94B. Detail of frame.
Lady Lever Art Gallery.

95. Convex mirror in carved gilt frame; *c.* 1800.
Victoria and Albert Museum.

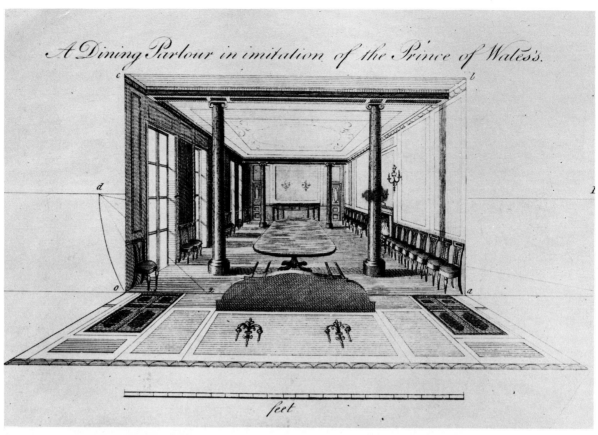

A Dining Parlour in imitation of the Prince of Wales's.

feet

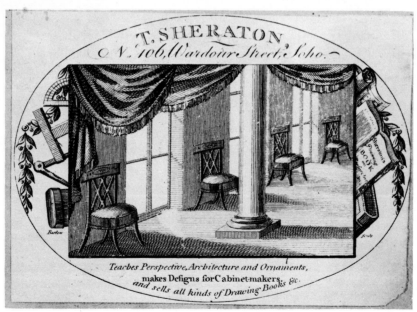

96A. Engraved design from the *Drawing Book* for 'A Dining Parlour';
dated 1793.
96B. Sheraton's Trade Card; *c.* 1795–1800.
British Museum.